THE CHURCH OF OMNIVOROUS LIGHT

Robert Wrigley was born in 1951 in East St Louis, Illinois. He was drafted in 1971, but later discharged as a conscientious objector. The first in his family to graduate from college, and the first male for generations to escape work in a coal mine, Wrigley earned his MFA from the University of Montana. He has been awarded fellowships from the National Endowment for the Arts, the Rockefeller Foundation, the Guggenheim Foundation, and the Idaho Commission on the Arts. He has taught at Lewis-Clark State College, Warren Wilson College, the University of Oregon and the University of Montana, and now teaches on the MFA program at the University of Idaho. He lives in the woods on Moscow Mountain, Idaho, with his wife, writer Kim Barnes.

His first book to be published in the UK, *The Church of Omnivorous Light: Selected Poems* (Bloodaxe Books, 2013), is a Poetry Book Society Special Commendation. It draws on several collections published in the US, including *Beautiful Country* (2010); *Earthly Meditations: New and Selected Poems* (2006); *Lives of the Animals* (2003), winner of the Poets Prize; *Reign of Snakes* (1999), winner of the Kingsley Tufts Award; and *In the Bank of Beautiful Sins* (1995), winner of the San Francisco Poetry Center Book Award and finalist for the Lenore Marshall Award from the Academy of American Poets. Wrigley has also won the J. Howard and Barbara M.J. Wood Prize, *Poetry* magazine's Frederick Bock Prize, the Poetry Society of America's Celia B. Wagner Award, *Poetry Northwest*'s Theodore Roethke Award, and six Pushcart Prizes.

ROBERT WRIGLEY

The Church of Omnivorous Light

SELECTED POEMS

BLOODAXE BOOKS

Copyright © Robert Wrigley
1979, 1986, 1991, 1995, 1999, 2003, 2006, 2010, 2013

ISBN: 978 1 85224 966 3

First published in 2013 by
Bloodaxe Books Ltd,
Highgreen,
Tarset,
Northumberland NE48 1RP

www.bloodaxebooks.com
For further information about Bloodaxe titles
please visit our website or write to
the above address for a catalogue.

Supported using public funding by
**ARTS COUNCIL
ENGLAND**

Cover design: Neil Astley & Pamela Robertson-Pearce.

Printed in Great Britain by
Bell & Bain Limited, Glasgow, Scotland.

to the memory of Richard Hugo

ACKNOWLEDGEMENTS

Selected poems are taken from the following volumes: *The Sinking of Clay City* (Port Townsend, WA: Copper Canyon Press, 1979), *Moon in a Mason Jar* (Urbana, IL: University of Illinois Press, 1986), *What My Father Believed* (Urbana, IL: University of Illinois Press, 1991), *In the Bank of Beautiful Sins* (New York: Penguin Books, 1995), *Reign of Snakes* (New York, Penguin Books, 1999), *Lives of the Animals* (New York: Penguin Books, 2003), *Earthly Meditations: New and Selected Poems* (New York: Penguin Books, 2006) and *Beautiful Country* (New York: Penguin Books, 2010).

All the poems in the section entitled 'New Poems' appeared in *Earthly Meditations: New and Selected Poems* (2006), except for the following: 'Babel' first appeared in *The Georgia Review*; 'Anatomy of Melancholy' and 'Soundings' first appeared in *Poetry*; 'Stop and Listen' first appeared in *Memorious*.

CONTENTS

Every moment of light and dark is a miracle.

WALT WHITMAN

The Sinking of Clay City

(1979)

Lull

Wind piled husks at the door
and made us sleepy.
Sacks of onion hung from the cellar beams
like scrota and swayed—
or stood still while we did. Two
miles east an oak was impaled
by a broomstick. In the west, houses gave in
to vacuum, the river frothed
and leaped, and catfish
studied the intricacies of rafters.

In the sifting yellow lamplight,
a few of us kept aloft
some desiccated cornsilk, a game
for the lull between thunderclaps, moments
before and after the only two hymns
we all knew by heart. And the wind droned on,
filling the air with crescendo,
with an organ's thousand throats.

From Lumaghi Mine

Dear Father,
     Eleven days without sunlight. We go in
in the black morning fog, work, and come out
having missed it all. But we begin to appreciate the dark.
It's too bright outside. Faces white
as carbide, even the shrill disks of real dishes.
It takes a day to get used to peripheral vision
again, the head light without the lamp.
     We rest after loading each car.
In that silence the seeping gas trickles,
as if we fished an underground stream for hours
without hearing water. So pain comes too,
when the muscles are still.
     I write while the world here works. By the light
of my headgear the pencil feels like a pickaxe.
The moon is my sun and the sculptures
on the dreamy mine walls shimmer into constellations.
I have learned how not to see.
     Sometimes I look down shocked by the whiteness
of my cuticles, glowing out of the nails
like slivers from an eclipse. They bob across this page
resembling fireflies or men walking a shaft with lip lamps.
And the worn shovels, the hands, hang alongside
the body, coal dust healed into the calluses. They seem odd,
astir in the milky bedclothes like frail, discolored spoons.
     Father, we are all the same. Dust fills in
the oldest wrinkles, the deepest scars. You see,
I am blackening—gray knuckles,
ears silting over. My eyes
are as black as anthracite. The sun could ignite them
and they would burn for days.

Coroner's Report

I begin again. There is so much
relief, but it is geological, the whorls
and contours of the skin shaded, exaggerated,
as though all the body had been fingerprinted.
But here, left hand ring finger bears
a pale white scar beneath the wedding band,
slightly green, from sulfur, or impure gold.
The pupils are dilated. Often, after the instant
of death, the eyes go on reaching,
glaring into the back of the lids. Always
it is the same unraveling: each man's life
a callous, the skin like cowhide, eyes
honed on a whetstone of darkness. And where
is the fat? There are only these lobes of bicep,
the taut cords of sinew and tendon. Inside the bones
have bent and gelled the color
or creosote, heavy and hard as ironwood.
In its jar a miner's brain matches the gray
matter of the banker. The stomach has grown strong
gripping on itself, and the heart has learned
all its possible rhythms: pick and pulley,
shovel, crack of tie and timber. Somewhere
loved ones are waiting for explanations,
a reprieve, some new reason for dying.
But this is all: these two hard pods
of breath, curse and cry caught in fossils.
These lungs, and thousands more, seeded on the hillside
like rhinestones.

Moon in a Mason Jar

(1986)

Moonlight: Chickens on the Road

Called out of dream by the pitch and screech,
I awoke to see my mother's hair
set free of its pincurls, springing out
into the still and hurtling air
above the front seat and just as suddenly gone.
The space around us twisted,
and in the instant before the crash
I heard the bubbling of the chickens,
the homely racket they make at all speeds,
signifying calm, resignation, oblivion.

And I listened. All through the slash
and clatter, the rake of steel, shatter of glass,
I listened, and what came
was a blizzard moan in the wind, a wail
of wreckage, severed hoses and lives,
a storm of loose feathers, and in the final
whirl approximating calm, the cluck
and fracas of the birds. I crawled
on hands and knees where a window should
have been and rose uneven

in November dusk. Wind blew
a snow of down, and rows of it quivered along
the shoulder. One thin stream of blood
oozed, flocked in feathers.
This was in the Ozarks, on a road curving miles
around Missouri, and as far as I could
see, no light flickered through the timber,
no mail box leaned the flag
of itself toward pavement, no cars
seemed ever likely to come along.

So I walked, circled the darkening disaster
my life had come to, and cried.
I cried for my family there,
knotted in the snarl of metal and glass;
for the farmer, looking dead, half in
and half out of his windshield; and for myself,
ambling barefoot through the jeweled debris,
glass slitting little blood-stars in my soles,
my arm hung loose at the elbow
and whispering its prophecies of pain.

Around and around the tilted car
and steaming truck, around the heap
of exploded crates, the smears and small hunks
of chicken and straw. Through
an hour of loneliness and fear
I walked, in the almost black of Ozark night,
the moon just now burning into Missouri.
Behind me, the chickens followed my lead,
some fully upright, pecking

the dim pavement for suet or seed,
some half-hobbled by their wounds, worthless wings
fluttering in the effort. The faintest
light turned their feathers phosphorescent,
and as I watched they came on, as though they believed
me some savior, some highwayman
or commando come to save them the last night
of their clucking lives. This, they must have
believed, was the end they'd always heard of,
this the rendering more efficient than the axe,

the execution more anonymous than
a wringing arm. I walked on, no longer crying,
and soon the amiable and distracted chattering came
again, a sound like chuckling, or the backward such
of hard laughter. And we walked
to the cadence their clucking called,
a small boy towing a cloud around a scene
of death, coming round and round
like a dream, or a mountain road,
like a pincurl, like pulse, like life.

Heart Attack

Throwing his small, blond son
into the air, he begins to feel it,
a slow-motion quivering, some part
broken loose and throbbing with its own pulse,
like the cock's involuntary leaping
toward whatever shadow looms in front.

It is below his left shoulder-blade,
a blip regular as radar, and he thinks of wings
and flight, his son's straight soar and fall
out of and into his high-held hands.
He is amused by the quick change
on the boy's little face: from the joy

of release and catch, to the near terror
at apex. It is the same with every throw.
And every throw comes without
his knowing. Nor his son's. Again
and again, the rise and fall, like breathing,
again the joy and fear, squeal and laughter,

until the world becomes a swarm of shapes
around him, and his arms
go leaden and prickled, and he knows
the sound is no longer laughter
but wheezing, knows he holds his son
in his arms and has not let him fly

upward for many long moments now.
He is on his knees, as his son stands,
supporting him, the look in the child's face
something the man has seen before:
not fear, not joy, not even misunderstanding,
but the quick knowledge sons

must come to, at some age
when everything else is put aside—
the knowledge of death, the stench
of mortality—that fraction of an instant
even a child can know, when
his father does not mean to leave, but goes.

The Beliefs of a Horse

In the field out back
there are some sheep, fat
and unsheared; two heifers;
and a pinto horse, his spots
like a map of continental drift.
One day soon a man will come
with his pistol and his high-backed
truck and take away the sheep
and the heifers, leaving
around the gate the steaming piles
of viscera, blood gathering
at the low point in a slow
and thickening rivulet.
The fence rail will fill up
with ravens. The air will throb
with bluebottle flies.
While all this time the horse
will merely stand, waiting for his
day on the trail,
as still as he can, monumental,
barely breathing, believing
among the flickers of leaves,
the slow-passing cloud shadows,
that he is lost
on the earth's great sea, that he is an island
the breeze quietly laps
and the sun passes by in its current,
the fence a near horizon,
that will someday break wide with sails.

Torch Songs

I would speak of that grief
perfected by the saxophone, the slow
muted trombone, the low, unforgettable cornet.
Theirs were the paths we followed
into the sexual forest, the witch's spellbound cabin,
the national anthems of longing.

Rhythm is the plod of the human heart,
that aimless walker down deserted streets
at midnight, where a tavern's neon keeps the pulse.
A horn man licks the blood
in tow, heavy and smooth,
and a song in is in the veins like whiskey.

Does it matter then that men have written
the heartbreaks women make hurt?
that Holiday and Washington sang for one
but to the other? Or is everything equal
is the testimonies of power and loss?
Is the writer the body, the singer the soul?

Now your eyes are closed,
your head leaned back and off to one side.
Living is a slow dance you know
you're dreaming, but the chill at your neck
is real, the soft slow breathing
of someone you will always love.

Skull of a Snowshoe Hare

I found it in the woods, moss-mottled,
hung at the jaws by a filament
of leathery flesh. We have painted it
with Chlorox, bleached it
in that chemical sun, boiled loose
the last tatters of tissue,
and made of it an heirloom,
a trophy, a thing that lasts, death's
little emissary to an eight-year-old boy.

What should it mean to us now
in its moon-white vigil on the desk?
Light from the hallway makes it loom
puffball brilliant, and I look.
For no good reason but longing
I am here in your room,
straightening the covers, moving a toy,
and lightly stroking your head,
those actions I have learned to live by.

If we relish the artifacts of death,
it's for a sign that life goes on
without us. On the mountains snows
we've seen the hare's limited hieroglyphics,
his signature again and again
we we've skied. And surely
he has paused at our long tracks there,
huddled still as moonlight, and tested
for our scents long vanished in that air.

We live and die in what we have left.
For all the moon glow of that bone
no bigger than your fist, there is more
light in the way I touch you
when you're sleeping: the little electric sparks
your woolen blankets make together,
the shape of your head clear
to my hand in the half-light,
and this page, white as my bones, and alive.

The Sound Barrier

1

We were in our beds or daydreaming
out a window in school,
or we were simply running, the fleet
childish joy of motion through a still, dusty field.
It was silence that shattered.

In 1961 I was dreaming baseball
when the bomb of air blew up. The bed
lurched, I raised my head to hear the windows
clattering in their frames, my mother's trinkets ringing.
And when I settled back into sleep, the room fell away.
There was a rush of dreams like stars,
the rustle of bedclothes trailing off.

2

At the end of its road in Illinois
my father's house sat cracking in the cold.
A light from the kitchen window shone
a rectangle in the snow, my father
at the table yawning toward work.
The sweep of his hair left a mark on the window.
He leaned to see. A high flash
crossed the sky, the brief faded wash of its roar.

This is for you in that airplane, the exhilaration
you must have felt, my father cursing you
for everyone on earth.

The Glow

1

Above the playground, from the hung-out
highest limb of a creaking, leafless elm,
the bee hive breathed all summer long.
A low sizzle high up, it grew
like the mound of mud thrown out
by a crawdad, hurled up
in wind around the thick and empty limb,
a great bronze breast hung sweet
above the faces of children.

The sky was it own
electric fence. Every high and wobbly
fly ball fell from its arc
as though swatted down, a egg shoved off
the sky's blue table. And birds
gave the whole tree a berth,
even the woodpecker, who strayed
from his place among locusts
to patter a while the elm's infested trunk

and flew away wild in swoops
from the dark swarm
the hive hauled out to halt him.
Only the wind moved high in timber,
its hiss across leaves
a harmony to the bees' wiry buzzing.
Still they sent out sentries,
who fought the wind's tug and toss
and wound up lost, stung

out from sinking their skewers
all across the enemy's invisible flank.
On such days, the hive heaving
overhead, teachers called
their students in, and from the windows
all afternoon small gazes flared
hard, wondering if this day would be
the last of the bees' lording over,
the high hold held finally in check.

2

Windows razzed with grit
and the great bowl of the playground
lay below the school, overflowing
with dust. All around them
darkened toward storm, and teachers
reviewed the choreographies
of disaster. Then came rain,
whipped in the sky to a froth,
spattering onto glass its

millions tiny scars. Here
and there a pane gave out
and the school sucked the cold
air hard. Halls filled with
files of frightened children,
rambling lunchless to the deep
and quiet cafeteria, some of them dazzled
silent, others sobbing, whimpering
for father, mother, sunshine.

They sat below the storm's
unmuffled engine, and when the walls
around them held they began
to laugh. The room roared
with the voices of children, voices

thrown high and excited by the wind
and their own clattering hearts.
Among such laughter and scoots of stools,
every child forgot about the bees.

3

Every one but the one who lived
next door, whose whole summer was spent
lolling in the cool near woods
and the playground's dusty spaciousness,
who daily gauged by his upheld thumb
the hive's expansion,
whose bedroom window caught every morning
the bees' first early dronings.
This one hid among coats and sweaters

and the day's hollow clang
of lunch pails. Knowing
he had only until the rolls
were taken, he slipped out soon behind
his classmates, dodging teachers
in their last-minute swings, and walked
out into rain and chaos, the world
aswirl with water and leaves,
with mud and birds and everything

but bees. With his left shoulder
he leaned downhill into the playground,
the school behind him paling to a hulk,
a shadow, before it was completely gone.
He looked down around him
for the minor landmarks a child
remembers, having studied this land
more carefully than any
textbook. But old grasses

swooned with the weight of weather.
There was nowhere a sign
he could sight from, no hummock of weed
that had tripped him one day, no bare
mark of mud where second base
or third had received his slide.
Now the slant of the land itself
seemed wrong, and he sat
in the thunder and rain, and waited.

4

Among the stone rumbles of the storm,
wind yelping through the trees and brush,
he heard the first low pop of the trunk
giving way, a wooden spoon
broken under water. The soft
mush of old heartwood sputtered,
quiet cardboard crackling, and then,
while the sparse crown swung silent
in its fall, there were only the sounds of storm.

It appeared black above him,
a wooden claw holding a hunk
of honey, workers, and wax.
He could hear the hive's
respiration, a million wings worrying
close and pungent air. Down
like prehistoric bird it came,
from a Saturday movie and nightmare,
and he covered his face with his arms,

and waited for the yank or crush.
But he was swaddled suddenly in tree.
All around him leaves and branches
closed in, nipping light and sharp his face
and arms, sending him a foot

in the air on the trunk's concussion,
and dumping at his feet, on his feet,
an offering of honey and comb,
gold and pearl all across him.

To his left he saw the ground a mass
of bees imbedded in their lives,
lifting up dizzy toward their deaths.
He saw against wet bark the queen
sealed in dollop, still and perfect
as an amulet. A few drones grazed
his anointed body, as though
he were a large and bounteous flower.
He rose and walked into the rain.

5

For a long while he wandered lost,
until the school rose up before him.
He walked through the door and passed
down halls littered with glass
and papers, slowly,
his feet clinging in their golden boots,
and descended the stairs
to be once again among the others,
children, and teachers, who only then

noticed his absence and turned
to the door, uttered one low cry,
and stopped. The eyes
of every adult and child
turned to the figure in the doorway,
his clothes frayed, heavy with rain,
his face a smear of small bleeding cuts
and drops of honey, winking
in the lights like iridescent scabs.

From his shoes amber puddles flowed
outward. All up and down
his legs was a fresco of bees,
mementos, souvenirs
fastened to a plaque and varnished.
The room lay before him
like a photograph, every face caught
in the moment's quick shutter.
He will remember them that way,

frozen in their stares,
peering up at the miracle of him,
not knowing whether
the look in his eyes
was terror or the transfix
of high wind and venom. He will remember
himself in their eyes, the look
that will not go away
for years and years

of his life as someone partly other
than human, removed, as necessary
and dangerous as a bee,
as chosen and blessed as any survivor.
In the halls and on the playground,
on the streets, he will feel the glow of gold
they have seen around him, hear the whirr
they heard that day, as bees
came to life in his matted hair.

The Crèche

It survived the loud, jostling train
from Baden to Berlin, and the heave
and slant, the pitch, pivot, and lean
of the bad boat to New York.
She held it to her in a hatbox
stuffed with husks, all across steerage
and Pennsylvania, down the slow road
of the Ohio River to Cairo
and up the dirt tracks and coal-
paved paths to Frankfort, Illinois,
her sudden husband, her life.
She was mined for the children
in her, one daughter, then another,
a short seam, quick to clay,
and not a single son to save them.

But each December found her unfolding
from their sheaths the pale
figures from Dresden: Holy Mother, mild
worker in wood, stock reclined
and ruminant, the infant peering skyward
through His upheld hands. And through the years
we have come to know this story,
how starved, buried on scrip to the company store,
the miner came coal-hearted home,
winter just begun, his daughters already asleep,
and the crèche below a sprig of pine.
How blind in the peripheral light, unhelmeted
to rage, he crushed the manger and the tiny Lord
in his blackened right hand,
spat the *woman* in her face,
and left that night and never returned.

There the story ends, but for one daughter,
who married, bore another, who bore
a son, who fathered three boys—two that survived—
and one that passed on the crèche,
the Holy Mother, husband, endlessly
sleepy stock, and the gap since then gathered round,
its eloquent absence,
its grip more powerful than any man's.

Appalonea

Appalonea Miller Voisin (1840-1901)

There may have been a time when
your name went unnoticed: Amethyst,
Hortensia, and Emerald Maisie Hopes
were your chums, your names
sparkling off the page like so much paste
and silver plate. The Chinese
say your are not truly dead
until the last soul who knew your name
forgets it. Somehow we misplaced yours
against remarkable odds: a name
like a bird that sings its own,

or conjures up music
and hard fruit. Winesap, Golden
Delicious, the loud applause of wind
in the dry leaves of autumn.
But not a single shining image
of the human face. Grandfather's
grandmother, anyone we both knew
is dead now, and rooting
through certificates and microfilm
we've found every vital statistic but your face.

So I talk, and your name
is the only answer. Appalonea. Apotheosis
of appellations, a plum of pure sound.
Apollo, Apollonius, Apollinaire.
The great Johnny Appleseed
who gave us a peachy cider, a press,
and a pint of apple jack. I'm drunk
in the swirl of your name, the way

it applies to everything I see:
that strong grayish horse
across the field: Appaloosa,
a portrait but not a picture,
a prize, a poem, Appalonea.

The Owl

I was young and leaned
against the gray boards, almost sleeping.
Newly weaned from the drill and splash,
the chamber-pot's porcelain contingency,
I knew just enough of darkness
and nightsounds, the musky aroma
of the outhouse, to doze there,
my nightdress gathered round me like a flourish.

When the owl lit, I knew it was God.
My first look from the door's
slim crack was proof: white
and blazing with moonlight, it lifted outward and made
in two great and silent wingflaps
the chicken house, dark and unclucking
across the yard. The black eyes rolled over
the lawn like searchlights.

Again and again it flew across
the still world, silent as a star.
Until once, as it left its perch above me,
it tilted and came instantly down
on my yearling gray cat. Just a flash
of talon, a gnarled leg of amber,
and both were gone, the winging silent as ever
across hayfields, the pulse of wings

a silver trail into trees. I ran inside
and shivered in my bed until daylight. Since
that day, I have wondered
how I came to be there, sleepy
and desperate in the stillness. The cat

likewise, yawning in its moonlight
meander after rodents and moths.
And the bird, the snowy owl,
winging effortless as breath.

Little girls rose then, and padded
out blinking, scratching, unafraid. And cats
have always been the denizens of farmscapes.
It is a world removed now
from my daughters, who still wander from their rooms,
sleepy and tidal, indoors, wakened by the moon.
I lie in my bed and listen, remembering.

Then I sleep, the dream taking me
away on great white wingbeats,
regular as moonrise, nightly as letting go.

What My Father Believed

(1991)

American Manhood

In the dull ache that is midnight for a boy
his age, I heard the sound of him first:
hiss of the pistol-grip hose from the garden
and the clatter a watery arc makes
coming down silver under streetlights,
on the day-warmed pavement of the road.
And though I muttered at first
to be awakened, I stand now in the window
upstairs, naked and alert, the cool breeze
sweet with the blossoms of locusts.

My wife moans and stirs. She is a slope of white
in the bedclothes, dunes of softness
below the light from the window
and single blind eye of the clock.
'It's just Travis,' I say, hoping
she'll lapse again into sleep.

I hope she'll sleep because he is a boy,
fourteen, soft yet himself, unwhiskered.
He believes he is the only one
awake, the only one alive in a world
of cruel nights and unbearable silence.
His parents snore, their house next door is dark.
He crouches on the curb
in just his pajama bottoms, barefoot,
swirling figure eights into the air trafficked
by insects and the fluttering, hunting bats.

Tonight he speaks a language I believe
I must have known, in the time before, those years
when a boy's body imagines the world, the heartbeat
rhythm of water on the road, the riches
coined by streetlights, the smell of the night
that is everything at once, alterable
and contained—all that keeps him awake
long after I've gone back to bed.

But before sleep comes, I listen, until the noise
he makes is my own even breathing, and I remember how
the old rented guitar I learned on smelled of music,
how the young married woman across the street
robbed me of the power of speech,
and how I wandered one night the alleys
of the town I grew up in, a brick in my hand,
breaking thermometers, taillights, and windows,
and went home and laughed aloud and wept.

His Father's Whistle

For hours the boy fought sleep,
strained against the whir of cicadas, moths
at the screens bumbling, night's
blue breezes, to hear out on the country road
his father's car rumbling in gravel.
He watched for the sweep of headlights
on the ceiling, a quick rush down
the driveway, then footsteps barely audible
over the lawn, his father's whistle.
Half a verse, a sliver of chorus, and his father was in
the house, quiet, the boy already drifting
in the night, asleep before the hand caressed his face.

It seemed to the boy that his life would be this way
forever, that out of the murmuring shadows,
the terror of distance, the danger of all
he did not know, there would come an order
like the one a melody imposed upon silence,
his father's whistle among night sounds,
as though breath, a song,
and a boy's simple fear of the dark,
were a man's only reasons for whistling.

Economics

He learned economics in the shade
of a truck, a flatbed owned by the man
he worked for, who owned as well the tons
of concrete on it, owned the farm never farmed
but mowed, the Ford dealership in town,
a great white house across the way, and a daughter
there with her friends, sunbathing by the pool.
A ton of cement in hundred-pound bags
he'd already stacked on pallets in the barn.
It was Saturday, after lunch, sun seared
his neck and shoulders, flickered
from the drops on the girls by the pool,
and shone in the suffocating dust
he saw through. Though his eyes were closed
when the kick hit his heels,
he wasn't sleeping. He was awake
and dreaming in the splashes and laughter,
resting in the dust and truck-scented shade,
leaned against a gritty rear wheel.

And so it was the joy he imagined
tied then to the owner's sneer
and warning. Joy, and the rage he let build
through a ton-and-a-half of lifting
and lugging, the loathing for a man
who owned all the world he could see
from high on the back of a flatbed truck,
sweeping dust into the air
and watching when that man came out
to the pool, soft and flabby,
and grinned through an oafish cannonball
that made the girls laugh, applauding like seals.
It was a rage that cooked in his old

black car, that ground in its slow start,
and lunged like its badly slipping clutch.
He longed in his sweat for speed and oblivion,
the thrum of good tires, the deep-lunged roar
of power, a wheel in his hands
like a weapon, turn by premeditated turn.

'You best work, boy, or your whole life'll be
as shitty as today.' When the kick had come
he flinched, involuntarily. His one knee rose,
his left arm blocked his face, and in the grit
of his right glove his fist closed on
the readiness to hit. He was ashamed
to be caught, ashamed for his flinch,
ashamed he could not, as the owner glared down
at his startled eyes, leap to his feet and murder him.
He was ashamed by his silence, by the ache
even then in his back and arms, the guilt
he could never disprove. The route home
that day derided him, maddeningly slow
through marginal farms and identical suburbs.
His mother's howdy-doo repulsed him,
and his father's little wink seemed the grimace
of a ninny. It was Saturday night,
he had no date, but did not sleep until morning,
when he rose anyway, hating his face in the mirror.

Monday, washing as always the endless line
of new cars, he began to understand
the limitations of revenge: murder, fire,
the daughter's humiliation at school—
these were risks he couldn't take. Even scratches
here and there on the cars. He cursed his luck
and scrubbed, twisted the chamois so tightly
it tore, and Sven, the old one-armed Swede
he worked with, shook his head and sighed.

'You just wash, Hercules,' he said. 'I'll dry 'em.'
So he went on, lathering and scrubbing,
quiet, Sven telling dirty jokes to cheer him,
analyzing the bouquet, the savor of women,
offering his wisdom in every field
until the boy threw down his sponge, spit,
looked the old man deeply in the eye
and asked in all his feeble goddam brilliance
what the hell was he doing here, washing cars
a half a buck a crack with a boy.

And when he saw Sven's expression
it almost came out, all the simply story
about sweat and mistakes, cement and rage
and the long ride to nowhere through a life
he couldn't stand. What would it have taken
for the shame to come out, the shame
now for wounding an old man, for kicking,
like any cool and flabby man who owned a world?
Instead the boy worked, behind him
Sven mopping up, silent until the last three sedans,
when he flipped the chamois on a hood and said,
'Here, goddam ye. I'm tired. You finish 'em.'
And so he was alone at the end,
when the owner's daughter arrived, brown
and gut–hurtingly beautiful in a shiny new car.
She waved to him and smiled, Sven was gone,
his blood sped in his veins, and he knew
she'd come no nearer to him ever in his life.

For the Last Summer

That summer with a thousand Julys
nothing mattered but the sweat on a girl's chest,
the sun's crazy blue weather, and a young man's
hands electric with want. The wind
above convertibles sighed in the cottonwood leaves,
the stars were stars, and the moon shimmered
in its own silver heaven. He was king
of the swath a train whistle cut.

Crazy for speed, he held the girl and wheel
and plummeted toward the bottomlands,
foundry lights ablaze in the distance,
and war let him the songs he swore
he'd never forget. That summer
of week-long nights, blossom-dark,
fragrant with dew and a dust
as fine as milled flour, he dreamed.

And his dreams were all glory and light,
line drives than never fell, his friends
his friends forever, and war
let him sleep until noon and wake
with the scent of his girl around him,
remembering the night before—
how he sang of a loss he couldn't imagine,
of broken hearts he could almost believe.

That summer with a thousand Julys
the sun going down each afternoon was more
beautiful than the day before, the factory smoke
vermilion and rust in its slant, and the night-
hawks like needles stitching the darkness down.
Nothing smelled as sweet as the gasoline
he pumped, nothing arced so cleanly
as the shop towels he tossed toward their baskets.

The world rode shotgun and reclined
on the seat of his car, lovely in the glow
from the dash lights, soft and warm,
and he knew what it meant to adore. War
let him dawdle there, virtuoso of the radio,
king of the push buttons, and all that played
for him, in the only hours of his life he ever knew
as his own, was music, music, music.

Sinatra

That skinny fuck-up, all recklessness and bones,
the one my father called 'feisty', was Maggio
in the movie, and in my twelve-year-old conception
of things, in the magical drive-in dark, I'd come to know
what was true: I'd found the man I'd aim to be.
Suddenly the fact that I could sing meant something,
and one long day of rain my father let me
ease from their even rows his dazzling
collection of records. Among the heavy 78s
of Gershwin and Lanza, I found him there—
Sinatra in a rumpled suit, hands in his pockets, hate
in his eyes, or love, I could tell. He peered
off the jacket with steel in his blood, with style,
while every song was love gone wrong, old tunes
blue with heartbreak. I believed his smile
was deadly, that weakness was ruin.
Five years later, still not disabused
of the cinemascope hokum, it was Sinatra, not me,
flipping off the nightclub bouncer, the fake ID I'd used
slipped neatly into the till. And tonight, twenty
years further into out lives, Sinatra and I have both outlived
those early days. The drive-ins are gone, and Gaslight Square,
and that bouncer, who grinned and shoved
me twice, out the door and against the front wall,
and hit me once so hard in the gut
that I knelt among the sidewalk crowd and cried, all
the night's easy beers boiling out.
There are whole weeks now
when I'm trapped inside the stereo's thrall,
when the old Sinatra convincingly sings how
love goes wrong. A little light turns the walls

to gold. I have solitaire, whisky, and comfort,
but I wake up empty. Daydreams run
my life now, and I wonder what sort
of man I might've been, what sort I've become.

C.O.

We left the quarter peep shows, the lurid skin
magazines and comical, unimaginable toys,
and headed down the block toward the Quakers, a fever in
us from freedom and fear, a pure joy
our first trip away from the army in weeks.
They were American Friends, in a cluttered,
postered storefront, and the fleshy peeks
we'd taken left us shamed and flustered
before their devotion. Out the fly-specked window
and across the street the Alamo hunkered in dust
behind its gate. Our counselors knew the C.O.
route, would mention Canada only if they must,
and showed in their eyes a faith I
imagined as big as Texas. I could just make out
my face reflected in the window, about to cry,
a kid who knew only that he wanted out.

First, they told us the rules: you must oppose
all wars and make no distinction between
them. No matter what violence goes
on around you, you must remain passive. Even
if your father is attacked by thugs, you
must say you'd only place your mild, beatific self
between him and their blows. This is all you can do.
Here the counselors stopped, took from the shelf
the book of regs, and read the army's loaded
catechism, and we nodded and they went on.
But maybe then we daydreamed. Already a code
our fathers knew, and the country, was broken.
I was twenty years old and could not tell
if I was a coward or a man of conviction,
didn't know if what I feared was a private hell
or the throes of our lovely, miserable nation.

And this is the simple end:
I pleaded the Christianity I've never believed
and got myself out. My American Friend
was a lawyer who drove a Mercedes and grieved
into tears each week at the list of the dead.
There was no sense in anything. And on the day
I got out, I went the Padilla, the Puerto Rican head,
to the quartermaster for paperwork and pay.
Padilla, from New York, beautiful and muscular
and younger even than me. We smoked dope
and I woke up chilled, clammy with fear
before the last sergeant of my life. 'I hope
you're happy,' he said, and I was too high
and frightened to know what he really meant,
but he stamped my papers, paid me, and said goodbye,
then I found Padilla, and we shook hands, and went.

What My Father Believed

Man of his age, he believed in the things
built by men, the miracles of rockets and bombs,
of dams and foundries, the mind-killing
efficiency of assembly lines. And now the boredom
and blankness with which these students respond
to the tale of my father's loss of faith sadden me,
as times before I have saddened myself. Around
the middle of his life, I baited him wildly,
hung in my room the poster of Malcolm X,
whose lips were stilled around a word
that might have been freedom, or fight, or fuck.
I remember the first time I heard
my father say it. We had argued and I thought
I'd won. It was the same awful subject,
the war. I see now it was never how he had fought,
but his countrymen. He said we should never expect
to love war, but to know sometimes there was no way
around it, and I laughed and said 'Just stop.'
In his eyes I saw what he couldn't say,
though right as I was, I could not
have predicted what he muttered. The rage that made
him flush and stutter and sweat was gone,
and only a fool of twenty couldn't see the blade
of pain he suffered, and suffered all along.
What should I say to him today, when the truth
I was so eager to embrace is constantly told,
when the plainness of it rankles like a bad tooth
in our mouths and the students scold
us both and naïve and thoughtless. What of Custer?
they ask. What of racism? slavery? the inexorable theft
of ever acre of native land? And I can muster
no answer they'll accept, but am left

at the end of class the argument's dull loser,
silent, contemplating the nature of instruction.
My father believed in the nation, I in my father,
a man of whom those students had not the slightest notion.

The Overcoat

The winter sun blinded, glass buildings
repeated the sky and all the endless traffic
trailed plumes of exhaust, white and vanishing.
I'd come out of the store wearing my new coat,
the old one in a box beneath my arm,
when I felt a hand on me.
He was old and white haired. 'I'll pay
you,' he said. 'I've got furniture to move.
I can't do it myself.' Around us
the topcoated businessmen flew about
like leaves and pigeons strutted in the gutters.

I followed him south and east,
out of the glittery district of mirrors,
toward the fleabag hotels by the licorice factory.
The air was camphorous, our breaths flagged out
and sailed away. From a street of dead cars
he lead me into a hall, smoke-dark
and redolent of licorice and urine.
Could I really not have known
what he wanted, there in the cold
and filth of that empty room,
when he turned to me and said nothing
but knelt as though to beg, his spotted hands
shivering? In that world unmade of glass
where the sun cannot shine, I knew. In that street,
that building, that brutal hall,
that room in which I gave away
what I had no need for.

Ravens at Deer Creek

Something's dead in that stand of fir
one ridge over. Ravens circle and swoop
above the trees, while others
swirl up from below, like paper scraps
blackened in a fire. In the mountains
in winter, it's true: death is a joyful flame,
those caws and cartwheels pure celebration.
It is a long snowy mile I've come
to see this, thanks to dumb luck or grace.
I meant only a hard ski through powder,
my pulse in my ears, and sweat, the pace
like a mainspring, my breath louder and louder
until I stopped, body an engine
ticking to be cool. And now the birds.
I watch them and think, maybe I have seen
these very ones, speaking without words,
cleared-eyed and clerical, ironic, peering in at me
from the berm of snow outside my window,
where I sprinkled a few crumbs of bread. We
are neighbors in the neighborhood of silence.
They've accepted my crumbs, and when the fire was hot
and smokeless huddled in ranks against
the cold at the top of the chimney. And they're not
without gratitude. Though I'm clearly visible
to them now, they swirl on and sing,
and if, in the early dusk, I should fall
on my way back home and—injured, weeping—
rail against the stars and frigid night
and crawl a while on my hopeless way
then stop, numb, easing into the darkening white
like a candle, I know they'll stay

with me, keeping watch, moving limb to limb,
angels down Jacob's ladder, wise
to the moon, and waiting for me, simple as sin,
that they may know the delicacy of my eyes.

In the Bank of Beautiful Sins

(1995)

Angels

Cigarettes pilfered two at a time
from her mother's purse, slender black candles
flickering all around us, dripping
a translucent, silver wax. Her father's
favorite records, Brubeck and Baker,
sailing out the French doors,
over the patio and pool;
her father's gold razor
sliding over my toes, to the arch of each
foot, to the ankle, to the knee, and beyond.
The skin of my legs tingled.
Over the fine bone china bowl,
filled now with hair and foamy water,
angels presided, a chain of them
tangled wing to wing
around the rim—in the too pale light,
in the artist's rendering—neither male
nor female but beautiful still.
We'd grunted the old cheval mirror
across the room to the bed,
and I could see her from both sides,
breasts and buttocks as she knelt
to kiss from my legs little ruby after ruby
of blood. A wedding portrait
hung above us, and two slabbed, mugshot smiles
peered from the nightstands—mother here,
father there, his glasses by the clock,
her night-mask in the drawer.
We didn't speak, we didn't need to:
the negotiations of young flesh,
this for that, mine for yours—one more coin
in the bank of beautiful sins.

I could have had anything
I wanted, and I wanted it all,
whoever I was, that peeled boy
so naked there was no skin
between me and the girl, there was nothing,
so that what I remember most
is the hour just after we stopped,
when she eased back down my legs to kneel
at my feet and hold my heels in her palm,
until nail by nail she was finished,
her lips kissing the air, her breath
coming cool to dry the polish,
an icy burn blown upward through my bones.
She rolled me over and lay down on me
until we slept. I woke
in the dark, to burnt wicks smoking
all around and a dream falling away
as I stretched, the weight on my back
only wings.

The Model

Last year, too far into my life
for it to matter, I learned how paper folded
into flight—a stubby, nose-heavy plane
that, properly launched, lilted a long ways.
And I was lilting too, a little drunk,
a little nervous for the wind blowing
in from the dark, and honestly frightened
of this tiny commuter plane—one seat
either side of its stooped, low-ceilinged roof.
Bent over so, I could not see the others
already on board, and I was the last one on
this nighttime leg to Coeur d'Alene.
How hard I worked, my studied nonchalance,
my legs crossed, and the magazine I pulled
from the seatback, something called *The Model*,
a hundred pages of lean young women
remote as the cold runway below.
I looked, while the twin props blasted the air
and blue lights hurtled off behind us,
at an article about breasts, their care
and maintenance, their myriad shapes
and sizes. Out the window, the city
must have paled and flickered out. Idaho
underneath its clouds hardly shines at all
with light, but with a moon-honed emptiness
strung between its outposts. And I might have
become more than a little interested
in breasts and tight buttocks, in starvation
diets, and limberness I believed
only the slow-boned province of children;
I might have slept, the ride above the clouds
straight and smooth, and the engines' noise a great
white wall of breathing, but the little boy

62

one seat forward and across the aisle
began to misbehave. He went rigid
in his seat and swung out his bony fists
at the young blond woman across from him.
He squealed and shrieked, she fended off punches,
refastened again and again his belt,
and clapped her hand tightly across his mouth.
Up front, beyond a pair of empty seats,
four other children—the oldest about sixteen,
the youngest maybe eight—spoke in sign,
oblivious to the caterwauling
behind them and the whole plane's numbing drone.
I felt a tap on my shoulder
and across more empty seats a man leaned
and spoke to me: 'You can come on back here,'
he said, smiling, nodding to the others,
all of them speaking, hearing, refugees
in the ear-shattering world of silence.
But I couldn't, for now the boy took hold
of the empty seat in front of him
and slammed it forward and back, forward
and back, making a loud, guttural cry.
There were groups of us then, little cabals
from the nations of the state of living:
the pilots, swaddled in headsets, consumed
with their lofty work; the deaf children
quietly reading, gesturing their lives
among themselves; the two hearing couples
uneasy in the back, now offended
as well, and in the middle of the plane,
three of us spun together in midair,
a vortex of nothing and the noise between
the walls and the sure enabling wings.
I don't know why I did it, what I thought
it could mean to the wild boy beside me,
but I ripped a page from my magazine

and folded a woman's lovely face down
across her forearm, and brought her perfect,
unimprovable breasts together in a vee and handed
that little boy the only paper plane
I have ever learned to make and fly.
He slung it forward in the cabin, into the lap
of the oldest boy, who grinned and might have
sent it back, had he not seen on one
elegantly folded wing a nipple
shining in the nighttime sky of the plane.
He nudged the boy beside him
but I could not see what they said or did,
for the wild boy alongside me pounded
at my knee, demanding another plane.
This one I made slowly, as he watched,
each crease precise, each angle examined
for symmetry, then unfolded it all
and handed it to him. How easy it was.
He was shocked at the simplicity,
unfolding and refolding it twice
until he was certain he knew. We kept on—
first the two of us, then the young woman
joining in—and soon all that plane
was a litter of crashed and glossy wrecks,
the heartbreaking, uninhibited laughter
of the deaf, of the hearing, hearing again.
When one plane at last passed into the cockpit,
both pilots craned around, moon-eyed.
They could not believe what they saw,
but pulled behind the curtain closed behind them
and made their long approach to the runway,
the airport, the hard world
about which, I believe, they must suddenly have remembered
nothing but the absolute joy of flight.

A Cappella

Sensitive fellow and bellower of brimstone,
our two preachers warred
until the younger—married, soft-spoken—suffered
what the congregation called 'a nervous breakdown'.
We mulled this over and knew
a line had been drawn. Benny left
for the Methodists, flushed with liberalism and luck.
Mark muled off with his homely sister,
Sunday school and two church services per week,
a lost soul sure to sell insurance.
So there I was, child of equal time,
compromise-kid, left to face the abyss alone,
the rib-rattling, stentorian doom
of the right Reverend Mr Christian J. Kuhlman.
But I could sing, so worked undercover, robed,
a godly doo-wop a cappella spy
dreaming of revenge.
                        How I found it,
slim trapdoor in the furnace room closet,
I don't remember, but shinnied up through
every Sunday for a month to squat
among the organ's pipes, doxologically drunk
and reeling with the heart-rattling air.
Through lattice I could see the congregation
chewing their gristly hymns, heads
bobbing in the battle with sleep.
I could see the righteous and the wretched,
the plump girl I'd talked out of her blouse
in the sacristy, the boy who would die
in five more years, in a jungle
the rest of us had still to learn.

And so it is the way with spring, old
Dionysian horniness afflicting the lewd
and the lonely alike: *This is your seed!*
the Reverend Kuhlman roared
to the catechismal boys, who knew better
than to giggle, but half-believed
the church filled up on Easter
for the bulbs of gladiolus, gratis and fraught
with the mysteries of fertility.
We made our glum procession,
junior choir in robes of angelic white.
Christ was risen again, one thousand
nine hundred, sixty-six times—
an avalanche of rolled-away stones,
a gangland, machine gun massacre of nail holes—
but we sang 'Today! Today!' a cappella,
from the steps below the altar
while the Reverend Kuhlman beamed
for the seeds we'd become.

After the singing, the procession back out,
most of the choir hung around the flowery foyer,
where crates of bulbs sat like arks,
but not me, easing off, sprinting around the building,
my robe and stifling suit coat flung in the bushes.
I leapt down through the basement door,
through the furnace room, and up the trapdoor hole
to the place of held breaths, the forest of pipes.
All the while he raged through a sermon
on sacrifice, I sacrificed my one white shirt
and plucked up pipes and switched their holes,
untuning an instrument seventy-five years old,
stuffing a pile of rags in the heavy basses,
sweating, wild to be back in time
and beaming, my hand held out,
hearty, hilarious, smug as the saved.

Lucious Hart, the organist, went apoplectic
at the first chord. I slid back
in time to see him, aging, kindly,
effeminate, fluttering down the stairs
behind the altar, his undone black robe
arcing out like insufficient wings.
And if I guessed the Reverend Kuhlman
would blame the Jews or the Catholics,
it was an honest mistake, the Crucifixion,
cards, whiskey, and the Communist Party
all blamed on them before.
But he didn't say a word, only stood
at the pulpit, his head to one side,
chin slightly up. He looked like Jesus,
shaved and beatific, neither bellowing nor braying
but waiting, until the wave of chatter
washed against the church's back wall
and returned as silence, then waiting a moment more
before closing his eyes and singing of God,
from Whom all blessings flowed,
in our church, almost a lament.

So we sang, and for a moment,
even those of us who had vowed
never to give in, gave in
to so many ordinary voices trying
to make up for fiasco, to believe in real wings, to sing.
Through all the handshakes after, the hugs and mugs
of aunts and great-aunts and grandmothers,
no one noted the smudge of coal dust on my cheek.
I was, after all, almost a child, dirt magnet,
dog tailed, my voice barely lower than soprano.
The Reverend Kuhlman's hand on my face
was a tenderness I might have known him by.
'Your gift,' he said to me, 'is music,'
and there was Aunt Betty, snapping our picture,

the one so many years on the wall,
then in the album, for years spoken of
humorously, then ironically, then worse.
It was the day—Easter, it was!—
when the Reverend took back his earlier prophecy.
No, he said, I wouldn't preach after all,
but would find another way to make my peace
with music.

The Longing of Eagles

No words can tell what they feel, how
mated for life they breed once a year
and no one calls it love, what preening
they do in the last light at dusk,
done for the good of the nest—pure, habitual,
the sweet uncomplicated essence of instinct.
No gestures pass between them, no eloquent eye
belies a hunger not born of bad fishing,
and the annual surviving offspring blinks once
at its dead nestmate, kicked over the edge and gone.

I do not envy their flights, not climb
or dive or the hover in a hard wind,
outrigger wings gone quiveringly tense.
I do not envy what we call their play,
the swoops and feints, the talons-locked
free-fall tumble in the sun of a false spring.
I do not envy their beauty, nor the keen eye
of the ornithologist, who can tell them apart.
I do not envy the air they fly through,
nor the waters that sustain them,
nor the darkness that once made of them
something rare. I do not envy their dignity.

For two weeks now I have watched a single eagle
troll the canyon, and this morning
I found its mate, talons and tail feathers removed,
a filthy hulk. I do not know if it is male or female,
but I would bet every word I love, the shot
that felled it was fired by a man. I wonder,
as he bent to his work—the hard jerks
at the feathers, the unsheathed hatchet

for the legs—I wonder
if the eyes were open, if even in death
they glared out with that fierce
dispassionate stare of the raptor,
the predator, knowing many thing,
but not hatred, not need, not human love.

About Language

Damn the rain anyway, she says,
three years old, a hand planted on her hip,
and another held up and out
in the mimic of a gesture she knows too well—
adult exasperation, peevish, wild-eyed, and dangerous.
But the mangy stuffed bunny belies it all,
dangling by an ear, a lumpy flourish.

And so again I am warned about language,
my wife having just entered the room
aims a will-you-never-learn look my way
and I'm counting myself lucky. She missed me,
hands to the window, imploring the world,
Jesus Christ, will you look at the fucking rain!

And because this is western Oregon, and the rain
blows endlessly in from the sea, we let out to play
in the garage, where I peer balefully
into the aging Volvo's gaping maw
and try to force a broken bolt, that breaks,
my knuckles mashed into the alternator's fins
bejeweling themselves with blood and grease.

And what stops my rail against the Swedes,
my invective against car salesman, my string
of obscenities concerning the obscenity of money,
is less her softly singing presence there
than my head slamming into the tired, sagging hood.
I'm checking for blood when I feel her touch my leg.

What tool is this, Daddy? she's asking,
holding a pliers by the business end. Then
what tool is this? Channel locks. And this?
Standard screwdriver, sparkplug socket,
diagonals, crimper, clamp, ratchet, torque wrench,
deep throw 12-millimeter socket, crescent,
point gauge, black tape, rasp—

but suddenly the rain's slap and spatter
is drowned in the calling of geese,
and I pick her up and rush out, pointing,
headed for the pasture and the clearest view.
And rising from the lake, through rain
and the shambles of late morning fog,

vee after vee of calling Canadas,
ragged at first, then perfect and gray and gone
in the distance. They keep coming and coming,
and pretty soon we're soaked, blinking,
laughing, listening. I tell her, they're geese,
they're honking, and she waves and says honk-honk.
She says bye-bye, geese; she says wow; she says Jesus.

The Bramble

Cathedral of thorns, brambly fist—
how do the snakes get along such thoroughfares,
that deep, spiny mind with no thought
other than swallowing the world.
My arms are crosshatched with scratches
and purpled by juice, my back flayed
like a flagellant's, but I'm not stopping.
The jars I filled with berries look bloody
in the distance—peck of bruised hearts,
glass vat of gizzard and lung,
easy picking at the thicket's edge.
Now I know what the sparrow's whisper,
those little breathy drums, damning and damning.
It's a car, old and black. Some odd blink
of sun shone off a shard of glass
and drew me on. I went to the barn
for machete and shears, for heavy gloves and a hat,
and now this shadowy corridor, this hallway of hooks,
this ramp of knives onto soil unwalked
in years. It bleeds pure black under my boot.

Packard or Pierce-Arrow, high-classed and funereal
in its prime, yards off and under
the canopy of canes and berries
nectar-dulled to a plush, velvet sheen.
The light itself is stained glass, the grille darned
with threads of thorn, spoked wheels sewn
to the ground like buttons.
Outside, a raven caws to celebrate the sun,
and the cane that falls before me cries,
or I do, falling back in a fire of spines
at the skull in the driver's window.

What god or devil puts my eye outside me now,
beholding myself caught and wriggling,
and the skull lolling over me—
one fat cane shot obscenely from its mouth,
another looped through an eye socket
and the third, smaller hole in the forehead.
Blood on my right arm, my ear sliced
clean as a mushroom, the first salt drops
purling down the stains on my shoulders—
I stop. *Hush, hush*, go the sparrows;
the raven still caws. Far away,
a truck's jake blats for a curve.
I loosen myself, on ragged limb at a time, and stand.

Five minutes, a few more cuts, and I can see
there are two of them, two bodies skinned
by the years and the bones inhabited by berries.
I would have thought, over time
some animal big as me or bigger
would have bulled in for such bones,
but now the light comes low, colored by sunset,
the canes red as tendons. I can see
they were man and woman once:
among the visceral thorns, the thoracic brambles,
a gold brooch and a tick tack almost touching,
having grown together over the years, or having died that way.

The porch bell's ringing. Supper's nearly done.
I'll bet my wife stands there a moment, shading her eyes,
wondering where I've gone to, maybe shaking a rag
off the leeward rail, waiting for berries.
Hush, hush, go the sparrows. The light is almost gone,
and I cannot move for thinking, and can't unmake
a tunnel out of light into light,
a door some wandering boy will enter
hunting for snakes, happy for the blackest berries.

But I try, making a weave
from the dead and the living, the severed canes
and canes unending, blood knot and brain weave,
while the bell from the porch goes mad at my absence.
I'm working now on pain alone.
Darkness comes down like a skin
to hide all wounds and bowers—
the graverobber's black suit, the lovers' abandon—
and if I make enough noise, half-bathing
in the horse trough, she'll hear
and drop whatever implement she holds
at the sight of me—slashed and bloody
in the doorway, my right hand
white and unscathed, holding out to her
a brooch of diamonds.

Cigarettes

All the science notwithstanding, it's still
a little like a kiss to me,
or what a kiss might lead to.
That first grand expulsion
of breath from the lungs hangs there
like metaphor given skin,
and we almost believe in ourselves
some new way. Now and then
I bum one, and the rush
of dizziness that results
turns me woman in memory.
Though I lived in the world
I hardly stepped outside myself at all,
and women seemed a miracle of confidence.
Once I crossed the street
to retrieve the still-smoldering butt
a high-heeled, tight-skirted woman had tossed away.
I touched the lipstick-tainted end to my lips,
drew, and the fire burned my fingers,
the fire she'd taken into herself and sent out
into the air around us like a spell.
The first woman who ever let me
touch her, a girl really, only seventeen,
kissed me so deeply I fell out of myself
and became her. In the moonlit backseat
I knelt upward and beheld my own eyes
in a body of perfection as vulnerable as a child's.
Quick-witted and foul-mouthed
ordinarily, she was silent now,
even as the moments stretched out toward pain,
even when I reached over the front seat
and took one of her cigarettes and lit it

for myself. When she moved at last
it was both arms rising toward me,
and absurdly, I handed her the smoke.
Maybe some tatter of cloud passed
before the moon just then
and in that moment her hands ceased
imploring and began simply to accept.
Whoever we would be for the next twenty years
took residence beyond our eyes.
With both hands she eased away the cigarette,
and the drag she pulled into herself
cast a light that left me blind.

To Work

The three-bladed, dunce-capped agitator pulsed,
and steam billowed into the basement rafters.
Monday mornings, in a broth of soap and clothes,
my mother wielded her stick, bleached dun
and blunted with probing, then fed the works
through wringers to a galvanised tub.
Those summers the neighborhood blossomed
with laundry. Sheets snapped and dresses swayed,
a shirt dragged its cuffs through the dandelions.
By early afternoon, by the basket load
lugged in, the laundry stiff with sun was spread
across the kitchen table for sprinkling.
I remember my mother's easy motions,
her thumb mostly over the bottle's hole
and the clothes rolled tight and stacked
like cordwood in the cooler.

And when the light leaned into dusk—
when my father in the gap between his two jobs arrived,
dinner done, dishes washed, my father gone again,
the tiny, round-eyed television squinting
over us—my mother hauled from the hallway closet
the rickety wooden ironing board
and began her final Monday chore.
I sprawled across the rug
and picked at the pills on the hand-me-down sofa,
the whole house filling with the smell of heat
and watery steel, the ironing board's creak,
the iron's dull thunk and glide.
Last thing she pressed was sheets,
one set for each bed in the house,

each bed remade in my sleep
before she lifted me off the floor
and eased me away for the night.

Then the night itself unwrinkling,
new sheets warming into sleep.
That last summer in the old house
many times I woke up late,
my father finally come home and collapsed
in bed alone, while I wandered the hall
to the kitchen, my mother at the table
in a bright wedge of light. I looked up
past the bulb on her sewing machine
at a thicket of pins between her lips.
And in my sleepiness it was one gesture—
her palm across her mouth, a shaken head—
and I was asleep on my feet,
hand in my mother's hand
as she walked me back to bed.
I don't remember ever arriving there,
nor the straightening of the covers,
nor the kiss she might have given me.
I don't remember the house we walked through,
nor the colors of the walls, nor the colors of the clothes
she labored over every night,
the clothes she made for herself,
in which, come September, she would look for work.

Parents

Old two-hearted sadness, old blight
in the bones, the history of sugar
and the daily syringe, show tunes,
Shalimar, car after car after car.

Here are my names, all three
trochees ratcheted out like comeuppance,
here my oldest living forebear,
the Depression, my nose, my love for jazz.

Let us locate our first marriages
festering in the cedar closet.
You show me proximity, I'll show you
the blank expansiveness of the West.

O roads, varicose and meandering,
bloody Kansas after Kansas between us—
there are days I'd kneel to kiss
the knuckles most like my own, other days

when a blue Pacific sun show me all
that's possible, whole oceans of air
I can dream myself a kind of prince in,
a kind of bird, who believes he reigns there.

Poetry

October, 1990

We're in a new state, and the dandelions
are strange, thin-stemmed and somehow sophisticated-
looking, a kind of botanical, West Coast cool.
But I notice the bees still plunder them,
even on his windless Monday the blossoms bobbing
an undulant syncopation I can't quite ignore.
The babies are asleep, and the heat when I enter you
is some true thing I'm dreaming, not a memory at all
but the body's one life, constant, expansive, simultaneous.

I can hear you putter in the kitchen, domestic these days,
and I admit, what I'm imagining now
requires your body, but not mine, my mind,
but not yours, the counter, the sink, the cloudy light
sliding from your shoulders and over your breasts,
across your belly, a drop of saliva of sweat
silver bauble on a hair and right before my eyes.

This life's already so familiar, I can tell what pot
you hold by its ping against the cabinet door.
I can hear the refrigerator uncatch,
its yawn of light, its full and satisfied hum.
But for some reason the weather's
gone and changed. Now a great flock of crows
rides a thermal out of the trees along the creek,
bees have taken cover, and upstairs
the babies murmur and stir. Dandelions sway
in unison, a decorous, chilly dance.

*

Listen, soldiers, I'd sell out the nation
to see my wife come in this room
with my skin on her mind. I'd pledge myself
to Jesus to see the light on her face
I might generate inside her. If she doesn't,
if I don't, it will have nothing to do with art,
or war, or the soul's blind abandon.
It will have nothing to do with weather
or crows, or with dandelions panting away
in the wind, having started all this unawares,
ubiquitous for the bees and their droning, yeoman imperatives:
the seasons, the sun, this great, odd, and unfathomable drive
toward the dark.

Majestic

The only word for it, his white Lincoln's arc
from the crown of the downriver road
and the splash it bellied in the water.
Two other passersby and I waded out and pulled him
from the half-sunk wreck, the high collar
of his vestments torn away for breathing,
a rosary knotted in his hand.
It's an endless wait for an ambulance
there, that serpentine road between distant towns,
night coming on, August, the rocks we laid him on
still fired by the sun. And so we came
to know one another, three living men
touching tenderly the dead one's body,
tending mouth and chest, making
a pillow for the head. He did not look,
we understood, like any man of God.
It was Roy, the mill-hand from Orofino,
who saw the tattoo first—no cross at all
but Christ Himself hung out, crucified
to the pale, hairless flesh by needles of India ink.
Jim, the prison guard, had see it all in his time,
and looked up sweaty from the breath-kissed face
only long enough to say 'Keep pumping.'
I cupped my hands behind the doughy neck
to hold the airway straight and knew
as the others knew there was no point at all
for him in what we did. After a while
we just stopped, and Jim began to talk about time
and distance, the site of nearest phone,
the speed of the first car he'd sent there.
Roy lit a cigarette, traced the flights of nighthawks,
and I waded back out to the Lincoln,

in the open driver's door
a little eddied lake of papers and butts,
where the river lapped the deep blue dash
a sodden Bible and a vial of pills.
There was something we should say
for him, we must all have been sure,
for later on, when the lights came in sight
around the last downriver corner,
we gathered again at the body
and took one another's hands,
bowed, our eyes closed,
and said each in his turn
what we thought might be a prayer.
Something huge sliced through the air then,
but no one looked up,
believing owl, saying owl,
and at last opening our eyes
just as the day's final light ripened purple
and the black basalt we knelt on disappeared.
In that one moment, that second
of uncertainty, nothing shone
but the cold flesh of the priest,
and on the breast, almost throbbing
with the out-rushing dark—
the looming, hand-sized tattoo of Jesus
we could just as suddenly not see.
Bless the owl then, for passing
over once more and returning to us
the breathable air, the new unspectacular night,
and the world itself, trailing beneath its talons,
still hanging on and makings its bleats
and whimpers, before the noise
and the night above the river
swallowed it all.

Anything the River Gives

Basalt, granite, tourmaline, the male wash
of off-white seed from an elderberry,
the fly's-eye, pincushion nubbins yellow
balsamroot extrudes from hot spring soil,
confetti of eggshell on a shelf of stone.
Here's a flotilla of beaver-peeled branches,
a cottonwood mile the shade of your skin.
Every day I bring some small offering
from my morning walk along the river:
something steel, blackened amber with rust,
an odd pin or bushing shed by the train
or torqued loose from the track, a mashed penny,
the muddy bulge of snowmelt current.
I lie headlong on a bed of rocks,
dip my cheek in the shallows,
and see the water mid-channel three feet
above my eyes. Overhead the swallows
loop for hornets, stinkbugs, black flies and bees,
gone grass shows a snakeskin shed last summer.
The year's first flowers are always yellow,
dogtooth violet dangling downcast and small.
Here is fennel, witches' broom, and bunchgrass,
an ancient horseshoe nailed to a cottonwood
and halfway swallowed in its punky flesh.
Here is an agate polished over years,
a few bones picked clean and gnawed by mice.
Here is every beautiful rock I've seen
in my life, here is my breath still singing
from a reedy flute, here the river
telling my blood your name without end.
Take the sky and wear it, take the moon's skid
over waves, that monthly jewel.

If there are wounds in this world no love heals,
then take the things I haul up—feather and bone,
tonnage of stone and the pale green trumpets
of stump lichens—are ounce by ounce
a weight to counterbalance your doubts.
In another month there won't be room left
on the windowsills and cluttered shelves,
and still you'll see me, standing before you,
presenting some husk or rusty souvenir,
anything the river gives, and I believe
you will love.

Reign of Snakes

(1999)

Reign of Snakes

1 *Revival*

During the heat of summer days, they sprawl
in the shade of sumac glades
or hunt the bottom-watered thickets—buck brush
and blackberry—dining on mice.
And beneath every yellow pine for miles,
the scaly, pulse-quickening sticks
from each tree's unlimbing.
At dawn and dusk you can find the snakes
on rock face shelves, basking,
sun still funneling up from basalt.
There are side canyon gullies, drywashes
and scumbled slides, half stone,
half soil, and shed skins blow in them
like a snow of translucent leaves,
while deep inside the winter chambers, a boil
 of approximate sleep, lidless eyes
unseeing, a fist of snakes as big as a man.
I stopped one night, road-drunk,
at the torch-lit revival tent
of a trinity of back woods preachers,
in Arkansas or the boot heel of Missouri,
where a graying, hortatory praisemaster sang hymns
of joy, and his stern wife damned us all
to fire. I rose to leave, filled with free ice tea,
a fistful of tracts in my hand,
then stopped, as the pale, thin son
held the snake above his head and began to dance,
the rattler grasped mid-length
in his left hand, the right
stroking the jeweled scales, a caress,
as he brought the head to his lips,
his eyes sublimely closed.

2 Confession

As a boy I flogged a cornsnake to death
with the limber end of a leaf rake.
It took a while, but I let my friends help,
and once, leaping crossways
onto the backyard hammock,
my head hung over the edge,
I saw the copperhead upside down
at the end of the ground's rush by.
Massive and beautiful, tucked among
hummocks of crabgrass
at the edge of a scar of clay,
it stayed there, tasting the air above,
then oozed away, machine of muscle,
machine of oil and bone.
And I have hacked rattlesnakes to bloody hunks,
grunting my rage, and made with a single surgical blow
a guillotine of the shovel's edge.
I have skinned them out
and exhumed the damp ruffled carcass of a mouse.
And once, I followed the aim
of my grandfather's cane to see one,
a blacksnake high on the scaly bark
of a cemetery silver maple,
a sign, he told me, of evil buried near.
My grandfather knew every corpse around us alive,
but wouldn't say which it might have been,
only tapped his pipe empty
against the shining, ostentatious obelisk
of the man who owned the mine he'd worked in,
then plucked a carnation for his lapel.

3 *The Fall*

Why snakes? Always snakes?
Why that long narrow room, nearly dark,
'Snake's Uptown Pool Hall and Tattoo Parlor,'
its phosphorescent fixtures shedding
a skin of light, half a dozen rectangular lily pads
fading down a swamp. Why Snake himself?
Buddha-fat, he sat behind the counter
dispensing chalk and balls,
and when summer's dank heat came down
he glowered in the exhalations of his oscillating fan,
naked to the waist—chest, back, and arms
a cathedral expanse of tattoos: twenty or more
curvaceous women wearing nothing
but strategically placed snakes.
My eyes adjusted to the dark,
but to little else. Already my friends
were gone, whooping their bikes down the back streets
and laughing. Blue portals in the half light,
my pupils must have loomed above my lips,
and the hiss I could not stop making, the long slithering
ess that was to have been my ruse and request—
a Slim Jim, a soda—now sputtered out
into a nest of breasts of scales, an evil I entered
saying less than a word. Snake looked down.
'You like my serpents, boy?' he asked,
and it would have been as though he'd said it
to the light, the door's wash flashbulb fast,
a hot crack of balls giving chase,
the fat man's dry hack of laughter behind me.

'You want to taste what's good, you got to lick
what's evil,' he tells me. Call it theology,
catechism, Giuseppe 'Big Joe' Truccano's
weekly hour of prayer for poontang
and heavy tips. His tie's unbowed,
a monogrammed handkerchief
covers his ruffled shirt and cummerbund.
He's the handsomest man in the world,
tends bar in the city at Anthony's slick club,
and claims the men's room attendant there
unzips his fly for him and fishes out his cock
with a spoon. I'm enthralled. We're at Toon's Bar & Grill,
it's nine a.m., and all the Sunday air's
a battle of dueling church bells.
I've skipped the service to be here,
for the communion of boot black coffee,
the host of a day-old doughnut, glazed.
Big Joe's got an illegal Bloody Mary, envy
of the half dozen jittery alcoholics around us.
He's got a platter of hash browns and pan gravy,
two over easy eggs and two strips of bacon
arranged on top like an edible crossbones and skull.
'Mama believed I'd be a priest,' he says, 'and I swear
to you, Junior, I believe I am.
I go down,' he tells me, 'every week I go down
on my knees and do the penance
the sin-shifter says I should'—
then the switchblade, sprung out
to hash his eggs and bacon in the spuds.
It's spring, the earth's salacious remains are rising.
Under the spell of his eyes the lewdest robins
are treacle, the long disquisitions
on feminine anatomy more beautiful than roses.

Outside, the last quiet moments
on the street, before the churches empty.
I have a minute, maybe two, to make it back
but I don't move. 'Go on,' he says,
and as I rise to leave he pulls the handkerchief
from his collar and drags out the medal
of St Christopher too, size of a quarter
on a silver chain he quickly stuffs back in.
It'll be all they have for a partial ID
months later, the pewter melted
under a blowtorch blast, the Saint's elongated
robes oozing down to the sternum, the Child unscathed
atop the flow, and Big Joe—armless, legless,
battered, even the genitals gone—
unfound for weeks in the tall grass
of some abandoned orchard, beneath a barren tree.

5 *Fellowship*

The men who made the railroad bed,
hauling off the overlay of rock and soil,
who laid the ties and rails, those men
suffered their wages and more,
now and then the great diesel shovel
unloading with a two ton bite
a hundred pounds of rattlesnakes
from a den, thudding on the dump truck
roofs and hoods like a scattering of severed arms.
They dangled from the rearview mirrors
and dropped along the road out of the canyon,
up Hank's Grade to the deep ravine
Lute Johnson dreamed he'd fill.
What a circus of slithers his garden became,
by the end of week one Lute

alone on his back porch just after dusk,
all the near distance before him
a locust whine of rattles, the contract good
for another nine hundred loads.
And before them all, the scouts and surveyors,
drillers and blasters, driving stakes
and locating benchmarks. They scoured
the untouched riverside, knowing
it would never be the same.
One blistering August afternoon a surveyor knelt
in the shade of a cottonwood grove
and sipped from a smooth basin
the clear spill from Pine Creek, so cold
it numbed his teeth and made his temples pound.
An hour's nap in long grass
left him plagued with a pox of ticks
he rolled to get away from. Imagine him
kneeling there, the burble of Pine Creek
a delicate counterpoint to his whimpers,
then Pine Creek alone when he saw them,
an audience of rattlers coiled
each in a hand-sized bowl of moss and rock,
looking and licking his way.
Or consider slick Albert Charbonneau, one-time powder monkey
from the Silver Valley mines, throwing the switch
and hearing the deep thunk, feeling the ground pitch
then seeing all around him, part and whole,
a bloody rain of snakes.

The word for her, I know now, was *florid*,
flushed and loudly fashionable Mrs Evy Weeks.
For years I believed conversation
embarrassed her, a sunrise reliable blush
boiling her rouge to the skin edge of blood.
Midday in summer, come to her door
for the one-dollar wage her dandelioned lawn
had earned me, I watched her pinch
from her deep, floral coin purse
the usual four quarters, her cat's-eye glasses
giving me back my waiting self,
her pedal pushers in gold lame
or the skin-taut, furless spots of leopards.
Her flesh seethed crimson,
as though the dark cool air rushing out
from behind her blew from a bellows,
the cracked dusty porch a forge.
She called me 'Bobby', the hated diminutive,
and bent toward me with the silver
just far enough the brink of her breasts
showed at the scooped neckline
and reddened in my gaze like miraculous tomatoes.
She was beautiful, I think, and drunk.
Every day at dusk her husband emerged
and eased his gargantuan Buick
from the backyard garage and waited
at the curb for her, then headed,
my mother told me, for the track.
Each week their trash can filled
with a glockenspiel of bottles.
By the time I was thirteen
our paths diverged—mine halting
but ascendant, hers certain decline.

Though there was that day, shamed
by my mother's nag, I'd put off her yard
long enough, and began a surly, mean-spirited mowing,
dicing paper cups and cardboard beer coasters
heedlessly, taking out the sad, swallowed pansies
with the weeds. The copperhead
was huge, thick as a man's forearm
and sprawled in the shade below a window.
I panicked. No other word for it. I screamed
like a baby and froze against the chalky clapboards
crying momma. Spiked heels gone,
her bare feet came palely into view
lean and muscled as a tree-climbing girl's.
Her left hand, bedecked in baubles,
dazzled the snake's eyes away
just as her right reached down,
took the tail, and in a single, brute
whiplash stroke sent a wave
through flesh and scales
that blew the fanged head off
with a gunshot report. Then she was kneeling
before me, stroking my arms
and asking me was I bit, was I bit,
and hold me to her, I see now,
just as though we were dancing:
her head on my shoulder,
and behind her the headless snake,
a helix of death throe coils
coming to rest in the just-cut, musky greens,
and her ear, in a fog of perfume,
only inches from my eyes, and red as a rose.

7 *Glossolalia*

Long interlocked ribly abundance scale
scatter racketeer of bead isinglass skin slough
slick back tuck of fang and spit
pit black waggle tongue strummer
air boil hiss and spin all din and kingly silence
Lord and belly-slither symbol O snake.

Rake ravaged hoed up buried in air
and blasphemed blackberry transits cartilaginous
coil and sleepless swallower of mouse
you peristaltic simpleton pure and perfect
pig feed demon O snake O angel.

Cottonmouth dirt phallus prey
of hawk and owl first mind fuck
and venerable venomous original kin
sin slinging charmed tumescent skin bone
speed of blood needy foil and oil
slick agent of doom snake man mask of God.

8 *Paradise*

But O you nefarious marionettes, limbless,
slithering brethren, and mouthpiece
Howdy Doodies of Hell—consider
the greater burden of
omniscience, that cold-blooded certainty
of absolute foreknowledge, the way
the Lord saith, knowing full well all
He will have said, knew full well
all He will have known. When the poet wrote
he'd sooner kill a man than a hawk,

I was not yet born, though I was well along
into my fifth decade when I saw
for the first time a hawk fly
over with a snake wriggling
in its talons. So plentiful the snakes here,
so plentiful the hawks, I hardly looked up
anymore, when a shadow caught my eye,
but did the day the hawk let go,
the snake in sudden spinning free fall,
my two youngest children at play in the yard.
Can you understand, Brother Snake, my swiftness,
all the old center fielder's instincts returned
as I leaped up and snatched the spade
from its spot beside the pumphouse and ran,
the shovel on its down-swing falling
only seconds after the serpent hit the ground,
not a dozen feet from where they played.
Some days, in high summer,
when just enough shade develops midday,
I can almost imagine the river below my house
the Euphrates, not the Clearwater,
and upstream, at the headwaters,
where the Selway spills from the wilderness,
a paradise, for all our doomed longing,
we've made a kind of park from,
where no one lives but the beasts
of field and forest, and all along
the sun-warmed canyons, your kind—
there, where I promise always
to leave you in peace.

9 *Resurrection*

The vast basaltic flows cooled to columns
or twisted half-set to a litter
of flagstones and cartoon wheels,
the earth today honeycombed
with caves and gaps, subterranean chambers
immune to seasons. All the better
for field mice and shrews, packrats
and meadow voles, rockchucks, ground
squirrels, and moles, a vast scampering
cornucopia for the snakes. In spring
a green wash overwhelms the world,
and sprawled among the daffodils
a gartersnake tinged, chameleon in the leaves;
or as late as Thanksgiving, lacking the first
true frost, the dry grass crackle and clatter
of falling seed may still unnerve,
the last bumbling grasshoppers loosing
a racket to make the blood go cold.
But never in winter. Snowed over, the canyon's
at last traversable, the only perils
sheer depth or snow-hidden trip wires—
fallen fences, a blackberry's creeping vines.
So this is fabulous, a sweet trick of fate:
a frigid day in February and a full-grown rattlesnake
curled to a comma in the middle of the just plowed road.
Ice ghost, I think, curve of rock
or stubbed-off branch. But the diamonds
are there, under a dust of crystals looming,
impossible, summer's tattoo, the mythical argyle of evil.
With the toe of my boot I nudge it.
Snow in the pasture is two feet deep,
a thermometer on the shed reads minus eight.
Mean leather, demon sap, I cannot

believe my eyes, my hands, and swing
the thing before me—snake saber,
venomous sickle, reptilian boomerang of ice.
There's nobody home but the dog
and me. She nips at the tail
and dances. If I threw this curved serpent
across the yard, she'd fetch it,
but instead I stuff it in a heavy burlap sack,
cinch the end tight with twine,
take it in the house and arrange it on the hearth.
Here's a cup of rosehip tea, a vodka snowshoe,
a cigar. Here are my wet gloves
dangling from their nails, holding nothing but air
in the shape of a thing—shaft, handle,
cylinder, smoke. Now the dog's asleep
in a parallelogram of sun, and one by one
a cold scent lures the cats from their lairs,
ears half-cocked. They sniff, they pat.
One hooks a claw in the woof or the warp
and pulls just enough to topple the sack
from hearth to carpet nap and jumps back
at the dim clack-clack inside.
Low in her throat, the dog rumbles—creak
of stone, light fall.
Call it Sunday, a day of rest.
I blow a huge, undulant ring of smoke
and wait.

Why Do the Crickets Sing?

Because it is not enough to open the door
or sit on the porch, I have to go inside
the clamor the crickets send up
after a morning's long rain. I have to climb down
from the birdsong heights, let the water
wick my clothes cold and lick spit
salsify dabble my neck and eyelids with its kisses.

The nightcrawlers' earth musk makes my dizzy;
they lie spent and glistening in the light of the clouds.
Now the bells, the bells! The succulent hell boil
clamor of their wings, singing the hearts
of the one sun deep inside the seeds.
Let us open the mud book and pray.

Even the slug glister looms: perfect firmaments,
polestar and moon, only now
my eyes too focus on the blur of the bells,
fingertip whorls spin sudden into music.
It is like drowning, chorus and string,
a billion breath-moaned horns breaking like waves.

Taproot is thunder and moss is rain,
the drum of it what finally wakes me,
or brings me back from some brink,
some light that held me down to pull me up:
or else it is the kettledrum rumble of the field mouse—
a shriek of terror, soar of the hawk descending.

Dark Forest

...and then, in dreaming,
The clouds methought would open and show riches
Ready to drop upon me, that, when I waked,
I cried to dream again.

CALIBAN

I love the way the woods arrange themselves
for my convenience: here's the stob

I hang my pants on and here
the shrub I nestle my still warm

underwear over, out of each leg hole
a leaf like an almond eye, one black

fly strolling the vent like a big city boardwalk.
And see how my shirt flung up

is the residue of flame,
a long smoke fading in the weeds.

I hear my boots go running,
though they will not go far down that ravine:

they miss my socks, one fist-sized stone
in the toes and thrown.

I'm ready now, dark forest.
Bring on your snakes and bears,

your coyotes singing praises
to my pink and nearly hairless flanks.

Bring on the icy night, the cocktail stars,
the flamboyant, androgynous sun going down.

Let my soles go bloody
through the puncture weeds and shards,

let my legs by slashed by thorns:
I will follow my old compass, slouching

toward the north. I will paint myself
in the mud wallows of elk and make my skin

a new brown thing. Give my eyes to the ravens,
my heart to the ungainly buzzard, its head

gone red over all the earth's
uncountable cadavers, liberator of the dust.

I bequeath my clothes to the unraveling jays
and I will, if I should survive the night,

rise reborn, my opposable thumbs
surrendered to the palms, to find

in a snowmelt puddle a draught
of the same old wretched light,

seeing as the water stills at last
the man I refuse to be.

Art

How the buck could have tangled himself
so tightly in a three-strand fence
was anyone's guess, each wire
torqued in a knot of barbs his legs, neck,
and new velveted horns were at the heart of.
He must have hit it full tilt in the dark,
momentum spinning him through
and in, every thrash thereafter
sawing flesh, by the time I arrived,
just past dawn, sawing deeper than bone.

From a hundred yards up the fence line
I could see his still occasional spasm.
The staples sung in the still air then
like lunatic clarinets.
There was nothing to think about here,
not for any of us. I was miles from home
and empty-handed, my pocketknife too dull
and small to cut his throat, and anyway, the way
he pitched and fought as I approached
might have left me dead before him.

I will call it a vigil then. I stayed and waited
until he died. At first the dog could not abide
the place and danced and whimpered
then found a pheasant's trail to follow.
I moved to where his one remaining eye
might see me and sat on a rock
among the new spring flowers and grassy fodder.
Soon he settled into the process, and the flies
embossed his bloody hide, and bile
frothed from the corner of his mouth, and he died.

Old man Behring, who owns the land,
notched the skull plate out with a bow saw
and sold the toe-head rack to the horn collector
in Reubens. Coyotes strung the guts
in a smorgasbord of coils and organs,
worried the haunches to bitten-out hulks.
And today, October 1, 1996, six months' weather
and the good work of magpies and maggots
have made this display, this sculpture, this door
the wind leans against, and one day, will open.

The Pumpkin Tree

Up a lattice of sumac and into the spars
of the elderberry, the pumpkin vines had climbed,
and a week after first frost
great pendulous melons dangled like gods
among the bunches of lesser berries
and the dazzled, half-drunken birds.

Then the pumpkins fell, one by one, each mythical fruit's
dried umbilicus giving way in a rush
of gold and a snow of elliptical leaves.
A skull thud, the dull thunk of rupture,
a thin smoke then, like a soul, like dust.

But the last, high up and lodged
in a palm of limbs and pithy branches,
sways now in the slightest breeze and freeze
after freeze caves in on itself
and will, by spring, cast its black

leathery gaze out over the garden
like the mummy of a saint or an infirm
and dessicated pope. Below, where the others fell,
that seed not eaten by winter birds,
one, say, buried in meat and sheath

of skin, will rise. From its blunt,
translucent nubbin, a leaf trifoliate
and a stalk as succulent as bamboo, it will climb
blithe as a baby Christ up the knees
of the wood it cannot know it is bound for.

More Rain

an elegy

Indolent and watery, the nightcrawlers sprawl
four of five a stride, all the way
to the mailbox. The robin on top's a bleary orb,
a rumpled bird ball fat with reprobation,
burdened out of flight by the realm's false coin.

Nothing but wet fliers from the better life,
nothing but bills, advertisements lurid with bait.
Here's a card from my sister, where the water's not
fit to drink; here's a catalog featuring
a million dollar bra. Licking the pages

will quench a thirst. And the robin, so fat
he cannot rise when I approach,
coasts down to the mud of the road.
There the worm meat's strung for miles,
and nearby the sated cat, having neither conscience
nor appetite, maintains its vigilant wait.

The trick, they say, is in loving the rain,
the ghastly abundance of open-mouthed flowers.
Some of the worms shine and swell—pink
seductive curls. They want it,
slurs the bird, and the ground fog whispers, So do I.
Now the red flag has fallen, now the thin door has closed.

As for the cat, it was all sometimes too much for him:
a mate's scent and everywhere a clatter of drops,
the supple and too silent transits green weeds provide for vermin.
He sniffs a worm and looks up perplexed, a tuffet
of down in his whiskers, having mistaken something else entirely
for the sound of rain on the road.

The Burned Cemetery

Understand the years of drought, the vast expanse
of unused land next door, labor costs,
the bottle rocket some local kid let fly.
After all, the dead were beneath it,
or above, safe in any case, no matter what
you ecclesiastical stance. And anyway,
the fireline the bulldozer cut around the place held.
All in all, it wasn't the worst land to burn.

And those of us who followed the smoke,
whose houses squat nearby, surrounded by tinder and fuel,
have little to do now but take it all in—
the two plush yews turned blackened racks, each
limb tip gray and soft as the untapped ash of cigarettes;
the occasional knot of artificial flowers
still bubbling in the shade of their scorched stones;
the resident field mice thrashing.

By night, under the bright full moon,
it is a landscape Goya might love, a negative,
a photograph snapped mid-Rapture—every smoke wisp
a soul, every char mark on marble a flame,
and the whole blank expanse of grass
and weeds the night sky turned upside down.
You can walk among the stars where no one lives.
You could fall headlong to the roots on fire.

Prayer for the Winter

I place two pennies, one on either rail:
warm from my pocket they melt the frost there
then harden into place against the coming tremors.

The ties too are tufted white, and fibrous mounds
of coyote scat, and the next occasional spike
worked loose, which I fling like the others in the river.

A crooked volunteer tree offer up its last
or its only apple, hard and thick-skinned,
bitter still but sweetened a bit by the cold.

Along this mile-long arc of track, four springs
and four steep chutes choked with blackberries,
and four cold pools crowded with cress.

It's a black fly wind, all ice and bite,
and the usual fishermen have all gone home.
Trainmen hate those pennies. I'll hide

until the engine's past, hide again
for the obsolete caboose this short-line throwback
still uses. They hate the clunk and jump,

the eighty-ton shudder pummeling their bones.
But I want something to show for this day
other than a mile of awkward walking,

a wind so fierce and relentless the chimney smokes
lie out in rigid lines and vanish, and the only smell
is snow, snow, snow, like a fat and generous relative

coming all day but still too far off to see.
And when it comes, the lead cloud billowy and black,
the first icy spits will sting like little fires.

Already the downstream train plows from under it
and rounds the corner flocked, a thunderous cake,
a mile of steel, a birth-water umbilicus

harkening storm, and I, who must ply
the deadman roads and walk the skin-tingling
right-of-way corridor, I don't ever want it to stop.

Not the train, not the snow, not the winterkill wind
that blows and blows. No, let it snow,
let the earth go blind and the highway unlined.

Let it come down like sleep, let the deep drifts
extend their leeward fingers and the springs spill
into long random sculptures of ice.

Wouldn't it be nice, marooned in a frozen world
for a night one long winter long, home
where the fire burns the years and wind

sings its one note wavery aria over and over,
and we are alive, alive, in a place
where nothing matters but that we are warm,

where the children toss their gossamer
untenderable coins against the weather,
and never lose, and never, never lose.

Conjure

There is nothing of her body he can't
conjure—texture, heft, taste, or smell.
This is heaven, and this is also hell.
He can dream the way moonlight comes slant

through the window, illuminating breast
and breast, her navel a shadowy pool
he drinks the darkness from, her skin grown cool,
and her lips and her lips and all the rest.

If she were here, he thinks, and he thinks too
much, he thinks. He thinks too much when she's here,
and when she's gone. And the window's a mirror
he's all alone in. If he could say he knew

every night would be made of her, a thigh
in the true air, her long, elegant spine
blossoming forth from the clothes on the line,
he would have asked, he would have asked her why

the sigh of the evening breeze is her tongue
and the rose of his cast off shirt his hand
unfillable and trying. He can stand
and go and find her still-damp towel among

the morning's last mementos, and the shape
of her ear, a whorl on the pillow's white.
He can feel the whole weight of her at night,
and the weight of her absence, and her hip.

He would say when she's gone he loves too much.
He's immoderate or reckless. He cries
and laughs at his crying, his dreams are lies
he cannot live without, a drunk, a lush,

inebriate of skin and tongue and hair.
But reason has no mouth to kiss, no eyes
he dives in. His head aches. He is not wise,
but strokes the round, blue corporeal air

and conjures her painfully into place.
Most chaste of lovers he is, a shadow
man enamored of another shadow,
and the dark he is kissing is her face.

Ice Fishing

From open water at the lake's
unfrozen outlet, steam rises, a scrim
dim enough to turn the sun as round as a dime,

though it's still so bright across the snow,
so low in the sky it rings
with a ball-peen clang behind his eyes,

each time he looks up
from his augured hole in the ice.
Wind spins a spider-silk filament

of frost from the dorsal fin of a quick frozen
blueback, and blood spots
the snow around the hole.

From the darkening woods
two coyotes pipe and prate, the late
mouse they toss aloft in play, the same

they'll squabble over soon. And soon
the sun will sink an edge into the ridge,
and the wind will chase its tail

behind the trees. Then the man will stand
and take his stool and tool
for the ice and the tool

for the fish and the fish and leave.
Only the low, late coals of his fire left behind,
pinkening down toward pure black ash,

the hole already scabbing over with ice,
where the dark below blows a kiss to night,
by the blood–freckled cheek of the evening snow.

EARTHLY MEDITATIONS

The Afterlife

1

Spring, and the first full crop of dandelions gone
to smoke, the lawn lumpish with goldfinches,
hunched in their fluffs, fattened by seed,
alight in the wind-bared peduncular forest.
Little bells, they loop and dive, bend
the delicate birch branches down.
I would enter the sky through the soil
myself, sing up the snail bowers
and go on the lam with the roots.
Licked by filaments, I would lie,
a billion love-mouths to suckle and feed.

Where the river will be next week,
a puddle two trout go savagely dying in.
Notice the bland, Darwinian sand: bone wrack
and tree skin, the ground down moon bowls
of mussels, viral stones dividing like mold.
At twelve, I buried the frog because it was dead
and dug it up because I'd been dreaming—
a fish belly light, a lowly chirruped chorus
of amens. I thought my nights my smell of hell.

Bland, humdrum, quotidian guilt—
if I've killed one frog, I've killed two.
Saint Rot and the sacraments of maggots:
knowing is humus and sustenance is sex.
It accrues and accrues, it stews
tumorous with delight. Tomorrow's
a shovelful, the spit of the cosmos, one day
the baby's breath is no longer a rose.

2

Dumb, would-be Siddhartha, I sat, lapped still
by the snowmelt rush. I was dull
as a beard and loved here
and there by mistake. The winter's last eagle lingered,
under its favored branch a garden
of delicate ribs. Air grew ripe
around them, like hands around
the heart of a prayer, the river a mirror
I was near believing: we are angels,
blue muck engenders a heaven,
this rush toward oblivion is the afterlife of all.

Somehow the frippery the cliff swallows sounded
escaped me. I could not imagine
the vaginal moistnesses of pleasure or birth.
That was the scream of a god, I thought,
but it was only tires on the highway above:
the beaver's spine dashed and rutted,
its belly-sides blown to bloody lips.
With brawny forelegs, it pulled itself my way,
blind to me, and tumbled down the rip rap
below the road. I wanted its yellow teeth—
it would not need them again—
so picked up a stone to smash its misery dead,
then heard the birds, their swirl and skirl,
their amorous warble in the fly-blown heights.

Festooned with their nests, the cliff
across the road looked mud-pocked. How the fissures held
and the nestlings clamored. How it goes
on and on—seed mash and the sun-blind
wings of goldfinches, swallows above
reproach, and a dying beaver writhing
on the rocks. Will my counsel have soothed it?
Did its soul come loose and lodge

in a sapling? I let fall the stone.
I sat. Where the marsh grass meets the sand,
where the wild rose kissed the season,
a hundred pink blossoms without a single want.

3

Plum and umber, dumb phlox spilling
from the canyon walls, its blue pinks deepened
each successive frost. An ancient rose,
a crone, sweet meat after meat for the bees.
The spirit dies a little, come spring,
each spring. Rib of trout, forgive me
my trespasses, forgive
my impatience with children, my curse
for the stinkbug and tick. I'm thinking
and thinking's a seed. The stillness
of the great blue heron is what I aspire to.
All the mud in this world is redolent
of just-cut meat, and nothing's at stake but the brain.

I am not the worst of my kind. There's succor
in that, though the beaver's gums are callused
as a ditch digger's hand and I am breaking
the laws of the state regarding game.
Slow as an hour hand the heron's leg
rises, the sun leans into its notch in the west.
My son calls from the cliff
across the river. From the drawn distended petals
of his mother's body, he burst
into the world and began to mourn.
The spirit took root in his cry.

Amazing Grace

1

Tick-tick, the clicks of the paper wasps
whispering at the window: I'm allured
and cured by the sun; I enter the light
celestial, my night cloak flares into smoke.
Silken travails, the day is knee-deep
in the transits of spiders, every weatherward surface
dappled by sacs—the pine in a winding sheet,
the broad-shouldered barn in a negligee.
That hornet's nest aquiver in the eaves, tissue
and comb, a comely, mournful hillbilly hymn.
My dream-sleeves ravel, my navel winks,
I am present at the advent of an hourglass of blood.

Here's mud in your eye, gentle dreamer,
the firmament's flagrante delicto, all the knuckles
of snails spilling their postulant prints,
hills made thighs in the day moon's boudoir.
The ardent prey, clutching his flowers,
a gentleman caller done up like a ghost,
bound for the lick of the cows and does.
The days are shorter and the nights are cold.
I sneer at the wasps' hysteria. The nest breast
wobbles in the westerly wind, the day
is a grave, its eight black legs atotter under the pall.

My dust, my yawp, my top-heavy blossom!
There's pollen on this stamen still, the sun
is warp, the earth is woof, my tusk's a tooth
I grow light-headed in the presence of.
Between the bull's mighty horns, the lacemaker's
done her work quite well, spinnerets radiant

and a dozen flies like whole notes
in a twisted scale, a rondeau. Ruminant
under such music, we believe we believe in the end.

2

These gray, nameless beetles, passing miraculously
through walls: the whisk of a swatter's no balm,
the ceiling's freckled with their stews.
And where does the sumac get off,
gone bloody down the slopes, late leaves
nearly black, like teardrops of liver
in the golden autumn grass?
My hair's blown back, my eyes are tearing,
the winds of the calendar snarl and bite.
I've got half a mind to think with
the worms. Rain's their affliction,
and we're here gasping in an arid year.

Only everywhere the bugs are reeling.
Last night I killed a cricket
with a glance: the cats have learned
to study the web-work of my eyes,
though not the youngest tom—all tumble and sprawl,
a sleepy rumble, a fish breath wretch,
like me. There's no blood husk in the ashtray,
that's a ladybug sucking some inks; the eyes
on the Io moth's wings don't blink
but weep. Where there's fire there's talc and dust.
The parchment nest wobbles like an udder.

I know these dreams are a ruse,
a camouflage, a trick of the eye.
The deathwatches click at my windows,
and weather undoes their orbicular book.
The egg comb inside is barren. Petal dumb,

I blunder, a dull unseasonable sun sets
the roof to ticking too. The whine of insects flying,
a kind of ooze in the air, the sigh
of the body's low flight, something peering
from the hatches like a child, into the caustic sky.

    3

Sweet Charlotte of the imperfections, that pig
is a groin on legs, a land mass of meat.
Say the man in the man is no longer
than a thumb, a cross section sealed in aspic,
head cheese of the head cheese, salt rime
in a hat, the pathos of an onion peeled.
I put on Arachne's prideful cloak. Not
a bad fit, all the gods in their venal dances:
I've skinned a snake, I've crushed a spider—
thank the wind for worser curses.

And isn't this some rube tangle in the end?
A rush of flesh the spider clothes, the night
before the first hard frost. Rise up,
mostly dead, note the filaments of liquid silk
in your first three-minute egg, spittle thin,
albuminate, noosing the fat blood bottle
of the timely heart. And there, scuttling out of cover,
the fiddleback arachnid sees its shadow:
it's like a dream, the first dream. Dark
beyond the confines of the skin shell, a thin, translucent twin,
walking on air.

Meditation at Bedrock Canyon

1

Unloved, unlovely, the bull thistle slouches
in the fields these days. It spills
its seedy tears and, shrunken, galumphs,
a dessicate dump the strumpet sparrows
spread far and wide. I'd die for an eye
like that, horse-sized and purple as a bruise.
I would lose the light and shake every shadow,
let the droop of my skin go
tacking the map. Oars of a boat,
my hands cup the musical waters,
the morning star sets sail in a spindrift of seeds.

What bird is that? The word
is the measure, the tongue
is the string, the flying change
of the elk, his majestic horns,
the delicate purple embouchure of his muzzle—
buss of blossom, thistle kiss. His piss
is rank as a composted heart.
How do the autumn bees dance
such desperate fandangos? The smoke
from a burn of stubble deranges their eyes,
and all pollen's past its innocuous prime—
stickum of whiskey, saffron booze.

That buzz is the muscular gizzard's grind.
Gray of the sky mocks
the pheasant's tongue. I've sung my seminal song
and dreamed the earth herself took note,
my muse of dirt, my mole hole umbilicus
to the dark. All the best songs

and symphonies blow the candles out,
there's a measure in the clef
of the skin and the lips. I'm a weed
and a weevil, a wing and an arc.
Anywhere I hang on is a home.

2

Friable loam alitter, the bulge
of the burrow's entry shaft, the uneasy maw
it makes, obscene, its badger come forth
snarling, some black secretion of primordial rage.
This is the forest medieval, stump plundered
and birthed by a hag, the swagger
of resource consultants festered in its slash.
Here the long rebuilding takes place:
blackberry scaffolds and the footings of stone,
a coyote's just-so scatter of bones,
probable gallows of a weathered snag.

That pair of ravens wobbling there—
Caliban and Caliban—they're drunk on fermented light.
They say I take my scars too seriously.
It's my Roman nose, the stupid clothes—
what's a mink without his fur?
I'll pass on skin I cannot kiss
and blow a thousand bubbles, little bobs,
along the stream. Who's minding the nest,
you beasty birds, what fledglings fail
by your profligate caws?
White as fluff, your shadows, cock and hen.

And the wren, aggressively puckish, preens,
its perch the dead elk's rack of horns.
All are punished and punished for love,
the first human wonder of the world.

Bloodroot, turmeric, bladderwort, puccoon—
call it what you will but bow
to its flower. The stigma, the anther, the sepal, the stem.
The day's eyes nod in a cool wind.
They are blind from the root hairs up.

3

The haunch of the fallen bull, worried
by a badger, twitches
from this distance. Brain weave
of a bramble obscures the tug and smack.
What new sacrilege is this, Walt Disney?
Where are the Hottentot lions?
the Yiddish cats? What language speaks
that widowed cow across the way,
mouthing down the last supple bloom in sight?
She stayed for the purple, she mourneth not,
I've reentered my clothes like a story.

Slump, dump, the green world sags.
I wish I could photosynthesise.
Summer's dark contusions—scab of knee
and plowed field, the peeled back skids
of landed logs; I sing a song
of loss across the sky.
I am myself and nothing else.
I'd welcome the sky in my branches.
From a night's long gulf of sleep,
my daughter unfolds and holds
all the light there is before her, and I am new,
the dew come down with its kiss.

Night Music

1

The bass drum ka-thumps, the snare's a wire
live with cracks. It lacks a rasp of its own,
lightning unstrung in the formless air.
And the bell of the horn? Who can bear
its nightly burden, its blood pangs
and the breath of angels falling?
Sky is not lovely without a light,
though just as the melody gives way
to silence, the body implies the soul,
singing the notes all around it.
Now dreary autumns of eternity go by,
miles of filings. Leaf by leaf, the tree
turns a minor key, its song gone back to soil.

I hear the sidemen of water over stones,
the skeletal chords of night bird cymbals.
Along this mountain road, the wheels
of the wrecked truck spin on toward stillness,
the driver's undone but lucky, kneeling
and sick in the ditch. Deaf, the gray sky glowers
and smokes, the truck leaned
at such an angle, I barely dare to move.
Posts uprooted, guardrail swayed out,
pulled tight as a string. I pluck it,
and for a mile the canyon fills
with a single, resonant, churchly note.
The world's afloat. No god is an island
in a sea of sins. The waves go on singing their way,
their way, the waves go on singing their way.

Things without voices, rejoice, rejoice;
things without hands, take hands.
The tune's the illusion, the horn breathes
its eminent brass into gold. From the body
of earth, the swirl of wood, the soundboard hole
in the canyon air, its rises. I am,
it sang; I was, it sings; someone else
will be who will be.

2

Querulous, the magpie asks, 'Aag-aag?'
Noise bag, contrapuntal cacophone, yes-man
of the nightly apocalypse. 'Song,' says the field
guide, lying. Likewise, the raven, papal
in his iridescent finery, regalia
of the unlapsed academic, going on an on without cause.
The song by God must embody all,
the whole scale, the baleful bawl
to twitter and giggle, love grunt and come cry,
gasp of dusk and sigh of dawn.
Who can imagine the painterly equivalent of Beethoven?
Some nights, in the deep, inhuman hills,
stars themselves go chiming.
In the pillow a blood-rush hisses,
rivets is a pan of spun brass.

Galvanised, the guardrail lit the truck lights up,
the driver looked but could not breathe.
All the needles of the larches, grown gold
with the cold, came shimmering down,
brush and stir. Drum put its ear
to the ground, the road itself took to humming.
Lively with leaping fish, the river grew.
What light was left was an aria. And eight slid-down steps

at a time, that one note vanished,
perking the worms, loosening the sockets
of mud-swaddled rocks, combing the hairs
of timbers and roots. Blind with eyes,
I could not hear the earthly riffs
and improvisations. I could not
see the harmony of its fears—that no one
would listen, that someone would hear.

Magpies jangled, the river poured on,
gradually water turned water again. Distant night birds
dithered and chirped. The whole note dome
of the dark came down, a passing
draft of exquisite music. A cappella night,
bow-skrick of cricket. Death rattle, black song,
a thousand solo requia per mile.
Inside my car, dash lights made a cloud of blue.
From the tape player, a horn
nuzzling the windows, needing the dark
far more than me or any man.

3

The locust's yellow leaf kiting down:
by last light, by glint of star of the car's silver skin,
it sank, neither love nor loss nor sign.
Down the wine-dark river
I drove away. Body, remember
that singing; hillside, recall that cry.
I am cupped and capsuled, swallowed
by the night inside the night. I want
the dead man playing in the spheres of woods
and water. I want the thing that lives
inside me out, aloft, borne up
and glistening, in a cape of rain.

Call the thing an owl. It's caught a raven,
sleepy, off the spar of a cedar snag,
the prey's black wings akimbo,
loud beneath the deadly skewer. They're a shadow
in the headlights, road unwinding to road
like a clock. Dear Lord, Coltrane's crying,
'Hear me out! Hear me out!,' a spot-lit illusion,
his horn sending flesh
to the sky, into the nightclub fog, into the night,
where a deep river sets its own music off,
into the passing afterlife of air.

The Name

1

The end of it, the start, a heart speck
flickering in the ultrasound. Around and around it
the smear of flesh, swirl of home,
a shadow, the spirit's limber bones building.
I slept on my back for years not to hear—
in my ear, some god in his robes contouring
the slope of a dune. He would come for me. I was doomed,
and I knew it. What feeble engine is this?
Ignition, parturition, pairs of arms and eyes,
all that delicate, permeable skin. You're in,
and that's the sin. All the rest is dying.

So they say, little cloud man, wing light pulse
in the sonographic sky. Why deny it?
The end's assured, irrefutable, and maybe not
an end at all. The call of your heartbeat
takes me deeper. I've been napping so long
the whole vast expanse of me tingles,
I'm dazzled by knives, by the waves
set loose in your mother's round house.
How's about a name for you, boy? a face?
a fate? Something to need, perhaps, above all else,
some pall that implies the brightest light,
a skin to love even more than your own.

Here is the dark and here is the day.
Where you live for now—in the gray wash
of waves, an inland sea and barrage of noise—
is all on earth you will ever know
of perfection. Gill-slits gone, fins

uncoiling toward a grasp, the genital array
lapsed to the single curse and election.
Your sister's more beautiful than all the stars.
You are strong and free for the incremental march,
until you bury me.

2

Cottonwood, cottonwood, let down your fluff.
The nests abound, plush as lactating breasts.
Clutches of eggs, all the thicket's adorned,
a hundred sacks of twig and grass.
In the spring duff, cottonwood, your root-sucker
others come greening into place,
the uprights and shoots. What an ecstasy
of fumbling the bees in your blossoms bring on.
A pygmy owl's knothole hoos
above my head, the rounds of branches
wound my instep and arch. It's March.
Bud resin musk coats the skin of the sky.

Here's an ear hump, a bass clef
mirrored and turned childish heart.
Now I'm carving initials
so far up the trunk, only birds and rain
will read them. I celebrate
impermanence, I personify the fire that is faith.
Blunt, pulpy wood, smooth bark
scarified by my hand, let this tattoo leak
down the cambium shaft come autumn,
let its birthmark enter the veins
and emerge, blood-sap and dream of leaf,
into the born and born and yet unborn.

My hair grows wisps, the catkins' shed froth.
Pitch gloves my hands with dust.

I have married a tree in the gold
spring sun, I have stated my love with a blade.
Cottonwood, cottonwood, let me down slow.
You know how the earth awaits us, my eyes
the color of somewhere loam. I am damned,
it's true, but holding on, darned to the tree
by the looped light threads all flights of sparrows
pull along. I believe if I fall
I will not fall far.

   3

Bud, then blossom; root, then tree.
The sap pulse of syringa, sun scope
pendulum, half the earth turning to watch. Swollen,
the labia stretch, the lips then the lips,
a swatch of scalp
and the arduous birth gush begins.
It's lush, a wonder, the redolent waters
spinning us aswim in the amniotic light.
From the womb of the hills and fields and forest,
from flesh of dirt and furrow of flesh,
a boy grows forth and lets fly his limbs
and swims again in the tragedy of air.
Where will he go? What will he pray to?
The latch at the breast is sweet beyond whiskey.
Colostrum's rich. They are blossom to blossom,
they are petals and pinks. The stink
of my sweat tinctures his breathing.

Little boy, little man, it's in you too,
current and spark, parent and parent and child.
Your delicate scapulas pump, the wings
of the circuit stroke the soul into being.
Cry and cry, tiny fossicker. You fidget,
the nut meats of your fists open out into hands—

calyx and fingerprint, contours of the earthly whorls.
All the worlds revolve in your name, revenant drum
in the valley of the breasts, and like the turn of the leaf,
like the sap's rise and fall, the fontanel springs,
a faithful code it receives and sends,
the word at last we all are known by,
where the cap of your animal hair pounds.

Lives of the Animals

(2003)

The Church of Omnivorous Light

On a long walk over the mountain you'd hear
them first, the pang and chorus
of their exultations, as though you'd strayed
out of Hawthorne into Cotton Mather—
such joyous remorse, such cranky raptures.

And you'd love their fundamental squawking,
little Pentacostal magpies, diminutive
raven priests. You'd walk into their circle
like a drag queen into a Texas truckstop—
silence first, then the caterwauls, the righteous gacks.

Someone's gutted out a deer is all.
In the late autumn snow you'd see the deacons'
tracks—ursine, feline, canine—sweet eucharist of luck
and opportunity for them all. Take and eat,
clank the birds, but not too much. It might be a while.
.

You'd wonder, yes you would,
and maybe nudge with the toe of your boot
the seeming rigidity of the severed esophagus,
gently belled, like a deaf man's antique horn,
and the breathless lungs subsiding to carnate blood.

You'd want to go, but you'd want to stay;
you'd want a way to say your part in the service
going on: through high windows
the nothing light, the fourteen stations
of the clouds, the offertory of snow.

Imagine the brethren returned, comical,
hopping in surplice and cassock, muttering,
made dyspeptic by your presence there, but hopeful too,
that something might yet come and open
your coarse, inexplicable soul to their sight.

Horseflies

After the horse went down
          the heat came up,
and later that week
          the smell of its fester yawed,
an open mouth of had-been air
          our local world was licked
inside of, and I,

the boy who'd volunteered at twilight—
          shunts of chawed cardboard
wadded up my nostrils
          and a dampened bandana
over my nose and mouth—
          I strode then

into the ever-purpler sink
          of rankness and smut,
a sloshful five-gallon bucket of kerosene
          in my right hand,
a smoking railroad fusee
          in my left,
and it came over me like water then,

into my head-gaps and gum
          rinds, into the tear ducts
and taste buds and even
          into the last dark tendrils
of my howling, agonised hair
          that through the windless half-light
hoped to fly from my very head,

and would have, I have no doubt, had not
      the first splash of kerosene
launched a seething skin
      of flies into the air
and onto me, the cloud of them
      so dense and dark my mother in the distance
saw smoke and believed as she had feared

I would, that I had set my own
      fool and staggering self aflame,
and therefore she fainted and did not see
      how the fire kicked
the other billion flies airborne
      exactly in the shape
of the horse itself,

which rose for a brief quivering
      instant under me, and which for a pulse thump
at least, I rode—in a livery of iridescence,
      in a mail of exoskeletal facets,
wielding a lance of swimming lace—
      just as night rode the light, and the bones,
and a sweet, cleansing smoke to ground.

Discretion

Wearing only moonglow
    and the fire's final shawls of smoke,
she made her way from the tent
    at 2 a.m., then squatted to pee,

and the heavenly light showed me everything:
    its cool tongues of silver lapping mountain
stones and the never-motionless leaves
    of aspens, licking her back, her hips,

haunches, and more, illuminating even the deep
    green eyes of whatever animal it was
that watched her from the forest then—
    a deer, I believed, and still believe,

though I confess I did not rise that night
    to make sure, did not shine my light or murmur
but waited, letting my head
    as she returned settle slowly back

down to the pillow made of my clothes
    and welcomed her shivering
back into the tent, from which
    I had sworn I would not look.

Sweetbreads

What foods these morsels be!
THE JOY OF COOKING

Thymus of the neck, and of the stomach,
Pancreas: it sounds like a pair
of demi-gods in Greek, don't you think?
Through lean times my mother specialised
in 'organ foods': the rubbery beef heart,
simmered several hours under pressure,
no less rubbery but having stewed by then
a good dark pint of flavorful blood broth;
pork brains breaded and fried
but in any cooked guise always and only gray;
the various livers—calf's on good days,
steer's on bad; kidneys, tongue, and even these
soaked, blanched, and quick-fried odd delicacies
once or twice: the butcher was sweet on her,
you see.
        Therefore, in my mother's honor,
I saute not just the tender liver
of this small but fine bull elk—
quarter inch slices slathered in onions—
but the sweetbreads too, pancreas (which means
'all meat' anyway) and thymus (which means
nothing but what it says), and in addition,
in honor of my father, who hated
every visceral tidbit she served him
but loved my mother beyond all sweet reason,
I toss in the unlucky bull's fresh balls
dredged in flour and brown them both up golden,
crisp and hot on the outside, warm and pink
cut in two. They bobble on the platter,
among the slabs of liver and wrinkled sweets,

like four domes fallen in a ruins of flesh
and fire—sweetbreads my elders understood:
all those dead dears who wouldn't waste a thing,
who at the scent of cooking meat closed in
and breathed it, who murmured as they chewed,
who kissed the salts from each other's lips,
then went to bed those nights thankful
and sated and blessed with a hunger
that would lead in time to me.

Affirmations

I am in favor of this pair of ruffed grouse
who in the midst of the snow storm feasted long
and obliviously on the wizened, bittersweet,
long-fermented berries of the mountain ash.
I am also in favor of the old dog,
who did not mean to frighten the deer,
and while I regretted that I could no longer watch
as snow accumulated along the doe's back,
I am still in favor of the path it ran to get away,
although its running is what frightened the grouse.
And while it is too bad that in their wobbling,
soaring glide, both grouse struck the window
I stood in front of and were instantly killed,
let there be no doubt that I am in favor
of the tenderness of each bird's breast skin
and the ease with which it tears and folds away
with its feathers to expose the pink, warm meat of the breast.
For I am in favor of this odd infinitive verb,
to breast, as I breast one by one the supple front
meats from each grouse,
these limp-necked birds whose meat
I am most deeply in favor of, quick-fried in butter,
with a skiff of salt and a rasher of coarsely ground pepper
poured on, all of which, of course, I am in favor of as well,
as I am in favor of the butter's hot graceful glide
across the skillet and the propane's dank waft up
through copper pipe to the burner of the stove
and the blue flame tipped with yellow
that blossomed at the touch of my match.
I am also in favor of the wine, and of the grapes
that bless us so many miles from their vines,
just as I am in favor of how the sun going down now

casts its light precisely through the gap
beneath the far cloud's edge—the end of this very storm—
and the lip of the turning earth,
and makes as it does an immediate billion icy rainbows in the air,
an explosion so blinding that for a second
I am staggered and take hold
of the kitchen counter, just as the house lets go its stays
and glides toward the night,
as though it too believed as I do
that at the end there would be another day
just like this one.

Do You Love Me?

She's twelve and she's asking the dog,
who does, but who speaks
in tongues, whose feints and gyrations
are themselves parts of speech.

They're on the back porch
and I don't really mean to be taking this in
but once I've heard I can't stop listening. Again
and again she asks, and the good dog

sits and wiggles, leaps and licks.
Imagine never asking. Imagine why:
so sure you wouldn't dare, or couldn't care
less. I wonder if the dog's guileless brown eyes

can lie, if the perfect canine lack of abstractions
might not be a bit like the picture books
she 'read' as a child, before her parents' lips
shaped the daily miracle of speech

and kisses, and the words were not lead
and weighed only air, and did not mean
so meanly. 'Do you love me?' she says
and says, until the dog, sensing perhaps

its own awful speechlessness, tries to bolt,
but she holds it by the collar and will not
let go, until, having come closer,
I hear the rest of it. I hear it all.

She's got the dog's furry jowls in her hands,
she's speaking precisely
into its laid-back, quivering ears:
'Say it,' she hisses, 'Say it to me.'

Explanatory

The hackberry tree, a static of twigs and branches
so densely woven sparrows went flitless there,
but hopped instead, stob to stob, and disappeared
like names, dates, and faces in an ordinary mind.
It was the bowl at the top I wanted to see for myself,
twig-sac of heft and weave, broad
as the hindquarters of a bull, nest of dozen
generations of eagle, heron, or hawk.
I had studied it for an hour and seen no sign of life
but saw a way up, beside the hackberry, up
the thigh-thick limbs of the yellow pine,
then out its long crooked pitch-dripping finger
pointing inside the snarl and bracing maybe
the nest itself. Even then I felt myself the fool I was,
in that deep green chapel climbing,
having lost the brightest light, seeing in every crotch of bark
a voodoo beautiful arrangement of rodents' bones.
I found the limb and sat it well, like a horse,
and skidded my way outwards, seeing from under the canopy of needles
how this mount was swallowed in the hackberry's thatch,
how the limbs of one had grown inside the other, until
on the last yard or less I was back in the open, half-blind
and wobbling to my feet, letting my bare, tacky hands ascend
the nest's outer wall. A single foot shy of the lip,
I placed my ear to it, a body of ribs. There was no heart
to be heard beneath the wind blowing by,
though by and by, my eyes at last unblinking, I saw
how just above my cheek a rabbit's skull swayed
in a thong of its own delicate leather, how the last round mound
between my hair and the nest's open maw
was a Joseph's coat of hide and hair. Slowly,
I stalked, lifted my right leg
and nestled it in among the tight-woven branches.

And there was nothing there but my arms, elbows locked
among the stobs and hoisting me up and up, nothing
until the horned owl came out flying,
leaping, hooked beak wide and blue-gray tongue protruding,
a mother-noise a million years old
that even as I fell, screeching myself, I kept on hearing.
It was her talon that tore the palm of my hand,
or a bone or a branch, it was something I held that held
me back, or seemed to as I fell, my legs
by the miracle of it swinging beneath me again,
so that I landed belly-down across the same pitchy branch
I'd entered on, then slung myself sloth-like from it
and dangled there, my eyes twisted shut,
my heart making wing-beat bird after bird,
my breath a mix of man's gasp and rabbit bleat.
And this is why my life and heart lines are joined inside my fist,
a kind of canal of the flesh, a path from knowing to faith.
This is why I have crawled along the thoroughfares of snakes
with a bedsheet, looking to rescue a broken-winged owl.
Therefore, when a grass fire swept toward it, I ran
to that same, swaybacked, fuel-dense hackberry tree
and pummeled it with stones and howled
until they rose—one, two, three, cat-faced and immense—
great horned owls aloft toward the going down sun.

Thatcher Bitchboy

She had brought home just a single white wing was all,
only that one through all the hellish August weeks
the fat man's chickens kept disappearing into,
and that one wing I buried myself in the manure pile
behind the barn, so that by the time he finally arrived,
Fat Man oozing from his high-backed truck
like a gristly hock onto the hot black skillet of the county road,
mostly all I felt was the least yawny pang of nerves.
I sat with my dog by the front porch.
'Thatcher bitchboy?' he asked,
and I allowed as how she was.
'Daddyhome?' he croaked,
and soon we all were there,
Daddy and me, that good bitch hound of mine sleeping
in a mottle of the day's last sun and shade, and the fat man
brandishing his blurred implicational snapshots.
There rose then a cloud of Daddy's might-could-bees
and a cloud also of Fat Man showly-izzes,
the sudden stormification of
which could have been why the sky itself
came on so holy and dark just then, a dreadnought cloak
I hoped the Goddumb damn dog would run off under,
but it was only when the light from Momma's
lamp in the living room window showed them there,
that it ended, and the fat man tied a rope
to the collar that convicted her,
and she licked his blunt and bulbous fingers with love
and servility ('tastez lack chickin doe-nit daug,' he chortled to the dirt).
Good cur hound, your eyes on me leaving were a blue
I believed the starved-blood likes of God's own ledger,
all the betrayals in all the lands of earth and more
recorded therein, a blue like the lost unredeemable sky

I would myself be forever falling into,
some heaven of hellfires and ice
I have since that mouthhot night learned to breathe in
as though it were the exhalations of the finest funereal orchids,
an air I believed would teach me at last
how to pray, and most certainly
God help me
what for.

Clemency

Over the trough, the long face of the horse,
and croaking dead center in a hoof print,
a toad—all the while the redwing blackbirds
drilling their whistly bells. February,
and a sudden, unearthly spring. God above me,
I am halfway through this field, a feeding,
the season, my life. If it pleases you, then hear me:
what I would ask is ten thousand more afternoons
like this, though doubtless the unkilled fleas, scintillate
and fat, will bedevil the dogs and cats,
and a few, skin-weary, will fall among
the rumpled bedclothes to catch us there,
my lover and me, and marry us done.
But please, just let this long light be garlanded by birds
and the garrulous, sloe-eyed toad.
Let the mare scratch her ear all down the length of me.
Let her breathe where the lick of memory wants.

Highway 12, Just East of Paradise

The doe, at a dead run, was dead
the instant the truck hit her.
In the headlights I saw her tongue
extend and her eyes go shocked and vacant.
Launched at a sudden right angle—say
from twenty miles per hour south to fifty
miles per hour east—she skated
many yards on the slightest toe-edge tips
of her dainty deer hooves, then fell
slowly, inside the speed of her new trajectory,
not pole-axed but stunned, away
from me and the truck's decelerating pitch.
She skidded along the right lane's
fog line true as a cue ball,
until her neck caught a sign post
that spun her across both lanes and out of sight
beyond the edge. For which, I admit, I was grateful,
the road there being dark, narrow, and shoulderless,
and home, with its lights, not far away.

Fish Dreams

She thinks the caught trout's eye must see
a monstrous face, for after all
its slick belly boils in her acid hand
and the hook's fluke knits the delicate jaw
half-closed. But I am not so sure.

Could you, so landed, understand
the majesty of God might live
among ten thousand types of fire?
Such beautiful meats we also might have been,
happily bereft of love and the black pearl

of emptiness our solitude protects.
Except she puts the hook and line aside
and enters the river and kneels there,
asking the current to kiss the flesh her now
flameless hands would caress again to life.

Narrow and cold the fish's world, and sleepless too,
they say. But think of the long night winter must be,
how, nuzzling the dark silt depths,
even a trout might dream of her—that hand,
the bottomless sky, the same terrible blue of her eye.

Kissing a Horse

Of the two spoiled, barn-sour geldings
we owned that year, it was Red—
skittish and prone to explode
even at fourteen years—who'd let me
hold to my face his own: the massive labyrinthine
caverns of the nostrils, the broad plain
up the head to the eyes. He'd let me stroke
his coarse chin whiskers and take
his soft meaty underlip
in my hands, press my man's carnivorous
kiss to his grass-nipping upper half of one, just
so that I could smell
the long way his breath had come from the rain
and the sun, the lungs and the heart,
from a world that meant no harm.

Winter Bale

Not a scent so much as a bouquet
of smells, that stable: old wood, horse flesh,
the round sweet buds of manure;
molasses, oats, leather, hay.

In the ancient bushel basket a nest
of twine, now the red taut plunk of it cut
from the bale, as puffed up
out of the flakes comes dust

from the fields a year before,
and a stiff, sleepy bull snake oozes
over the cold floor and into the stall
where the edgy stallion waits for hay.

Bridge

Red Wolf Crossing, Snake River

You must understand the river
was a river then
not a pool behind a dam
above a pool behind a dam
above a pool behind a dam
and so on
I could go on
but see how the flow of the poem here is likewise unaesthetically halted
though this was then I'm talking about
and there was no poetry then
no poetry at all
that was not spoken and spoken
chanted and sung
as the river itself might be said to have sung and sung
though that would be to personify to sentimentalise
to make of the river a conscious being aware
of its own voice
aware of the other-way rush of the salmon
which this myth would have as the first bridge

young Red Wolf and the woman he loved
and chased among the drying racks and alder fires
the woman who laughed
and sprinting left him flat-footed and breathless
on the shore
her feet so lightly coming down
on the broad silver backs and rolling blue bellies
on the rounded red sides of the sockeyes
that she was in his eyes walking
on water though nothing
made a god of her anymore than she herself

on the far shore
when she shed her robe and smiled and made ready
from which also comes the word redd
river womb for egg and milt
and Red Wolf or the father of Red Wolf
or the fathers of all men
leaped and began

and thus it is now
when the river is a pool behind a dam
above a pool behind and dam
and so on
that the surface of the bridge in the elegiac last light
sometimes takes on the colors of their original skins
and not even the most sadly prudish of men and women
can fail to see the huge erotic symbolism
of the bridge
which is after all only concrete and steel
an elegant and unintentional cenotaph
built so someone must have thought to further
the mercantile and industrial needs of nowhere in particular
where nothing much has happened
but ten thousand years of miracles
before the beginning of the beginning of the end
of time

The Other World

So here is the old buck
    who all winter long
had traveled with the does
    and yearlings, with the fawns
just past their spots,
    and who had hung back,
walking where the others had walked,
    eating what they had left,
and who had struck now and then
    a pose against the wind,
against a limb-snap or the way
    the light came slinking
among the trees.

Here is the mangled ear
    and the twisted, hindering leg.
Here, already bearing him away
    among the last drifts of snow
and the nightly hard freezes,
    is a line of tiny ants,
making its way from the cave
    of the right eye, over the steep
occipital ridge, across the moonscape shed-horn
    medallion and through the valley
of the ear's cloven shadow
    to the ground,
where among the staves
    of shed needles and the red earthy wine
they carry him
    bit by gnawn bit
into another world.

Beautiful Country

(2010)

Responsibility

(for Clyde Fixmer)

At the lower fence line under the stars
he hears what at first he takes
to be the neighbor's mare,
come to investigate his apple pocket,

but then gets that neck-chill
and knows otherwise and turns
to see by starlight alone a dust devil
spitting along perpendicular to the wire

and straight at him. He's seen thousands
of the things but never crossed paths
with one on foot, and watches
as long as he can before the grit

of its coming edge gets in his eyes.
Then up his pants legs and sleeves
the dust of it spins. His shirt wants to open
over his spine, his cap levitates

and vanishes, the fence buzzes
and rattles, its staples scraping, its posts
making a knuckle crack clatter—
and then it's past, back and forthing

over the pasture toward the hulk
of the old stable, from the roof of which
it removes three or four thin flimsy shakes
and causes the aged gelding BJ

to flinch and whirl and trot out into the open
and glare, with stars in his eyes,
at the man who is responsible
for everything that happens.

Hay Day

Beautiful, the nine-hundred-pound round
bale of smooth brome the grower and I roll
from the back of his truck against the usual tree.
The horses can hardly contain themselves.
They smelled and came running across the field
and now they look and nicker, and move in
even before I can cut loose the four long
bands of twine from the edge, where they nip instead
the greenest, sweetest stuff from the wound center
of the man-high wheel of it. They feed there
for most of an hour, long after I've written the check
and the hay man's made his way back home
and it being August I relax on the porch
with a beer my wife brought from town
and, knowing my usual routine on such days, slipped
into the freezer until just minutes ago, so that
I might sit and watch the horses, having had
all they want, move in slow circles around
the great black walnut's vast expanse of shade,
then stop—BJ, the troublesome elder, and Red,
the elegant, genuinely exceptional ride—
as always in the same precise relation to one another
(Red at forty-five degrees and a little back)—
before taking off around the fence line
at a trot, then a canter, and then, for just a few
beautiful moments, a dead and joyful run.

County

County of innumerable nowheres, half its dogs
underfed and of indeterminate breed. County
of the deep fryer and staples in glass against mice,
county of horned gods and billed hats. Sweat county,
shiver county. The hallowed outhouse
upholstered in wooly carpet, the sack of lime,
time out of time, county of country music.

Insufficient snowplows county, county
of the blasted doe all winter in a drift, dust sift
and feather duster county, county of the quo
all status is attached to. Of batches and bitchdogs
howling, of rowels and boots, of soot wash,
of the chimney sweep's red beard,
of the songless radio preaching to no one in the shed.

County of the deadly road, of the shoat pig roasted
in a pit. County of molasses, hobo coffee,
and sugarless soft-drink, county of the methamphetamine
picture window, of the padlock and massive hasp.
County of tools and dewormers. Curry comb
and salt block, black pepper gravy, red-eye venison,
blood sausage, county of Bud Light girl posters.

Treblehook county, chum county, bear bait
and dead wolf county. County of the coyote pelt
nailed to the barn door. Bruised woman county,
of men missing one or more fingers, single-finger
wave county. Pistol alongside the cash register.
Pitch-dense firewood county, county of the fearful
and fearless, of the distant mysterious school.

Target-poor county, Walmart holyland,
malodorous pulp mill and paper plate county.
County of the hundred yard drive to the post office,
oddly familiar faces among the wanted posters,
four hour drive from the county seat county,
unadopted highway, county of no return.
County of August always somewhere burning.

Beercan bejeweled barrow pit county, hardly
one bullet-unpunctuated county road sign county.
County of the ATV and ancient Indian trail
into the high mountains. Get your bull or buck
county. On-the-way-to-somewhere-else,
doe-see-doe, hundred frozen casseroles
after the funeral, go to heaven county,

blister and blister rust county, Jahweh trailerhouse
county, unassisted living, county
of the Gospels and the Penthouse under the bed.
County of tenderness and terror, of almost
universal skepticism, Jesus country county.
County of the cell tower stipend, everywhere
and anywhere, boneyard county, county

a day's drive from the end of the open road.
Softshell Baptist county. Pentecostal pancake county.
County of illusions and of hard facts. Rock
and broken shock, rock and roll aught-six
save your shell casing. County of not quite breath-taking
vistas, of the for sale sign, of timothy and brome,
spring and autumn slaughter county, meat county, home.

I Like the Wind

We are at or near that approximate line
where a stiff breeze becomes
or lapses from a considerable wind,
and I like it here, the chimney smokes
right-angled from west to east but still
for those brief intact stretches of them
the plush animal tails of fires.
I like how the stiffness rouses the birds
right up until what's considerable sends them
to shelter. I like how the afternoon's rain,
having wakened the soil's raw materials,
has sent a rootsmell into the air around us
and which the pine trees sway stately within.
I like how the sun strains not
to go down, how the horizon tugs gently at it
and how the distant grain elevator's shadow
ripples over the stubble of the field.
I like the bird feeder's slant
and the dribble of its seeds. I like the cat's
sleepiness as the breeze then the wind
then the breeze keeps combing her fur.
I like the body of the mouse at her feet.
I like the way the apple core I tossed away
has browned so quickly. It is much to be admired,
as is the way the doe extends her elegant neck
in its direction, and the workings of her black nostrils too.
I like the sound of the southbound truck
blowing by headed east. I like the fact
that the dog is not barking. I like the ark
of the house afloat on the sea of March,
and the swells of the crop hills bedizened
with cedillas of old snow. I like old snow.

I like my lungs and their conversion
to the gospel of spring. I like the wing
of the magpie outheld as he probes beneath it
for fleas or lice. That's especially nice,
the last sun pinkening his underfeathers
as it also pinks the dark when I close my eyes,
which I like to do, in the face of it,
this stiff breeze that was,
when I closed them, a considerable wind.

Progress

You begin to fear all the nowheres are somewheres now.
Everywhere's been discovered. Is there anywhere you can go
and find a hair-netted octogenarian wrangling a walker
and four massive, camp-sized cast iron skillets full

of Sunday dinner fried chicken at 9:00 am
and ask if she's serving breakfast, then have her say
'Sure thing, hon, but you'll have to wait on yourselves'?
Remember how pretty you were? Well, your sweetheart was

beautiful and all you wanted was some
sunnyside up eggs and bacon with hashbrowns,
a white boat of peppery pan gravy,
and a mason jar of homemade apple butter

you'd have to pry the disk of wax out of
and dollop on your toast with a long-shanked teaspoon.
These days Main Street features two antiques emporia,
a coffee shop, and a wine store offering Friday night

tastings of the latest regional Cab Franc cuvée.
The café's become an office dealing in view lots,
weekend lakeside rentals, and time share condominiums.
That was twenty-five years ago, you tell yourself.

The old chicken-frying woman probably never saw
what's become of the place, though what with the baskets
of brightly colored artificial geraniums hanging
from the vintage lamp posts and the new pocket park

with a memorial to the loggers of yesteryear,
she'd probably approve. There's a new high school too,
and according to its electronic marquee sign,
not only is there a girls' basketball team but they've won

the state three-B championship for the second time this year.
And probably the granola and yogurt breakfast parfait
with seasonal fruit from California's central valley
you had this morning was better for your arteries anyway.

Your sweetheart's still gorgeous and you're willing
to settle for distinguished or fairly well preserved,
but the jam this morning comes in those tiny single-serving jars
sealed with a stirrup of foily paper, and you remember

how that morning's apple butter was explosive with cinnamon
and cloves, how the tang came from the cooked
to submission red and golden mottled peelings,
and how the old lady wheeled and toddled

over to the kitchen doorway and called you back to
'Try this for a finish up,' and it was a plank of sweet cream
strudel still warm from the oven, a perfect square of butter
liquefying itself on top, and you and your sweetheart split it

and because of it all fell more deeply in love than before,
and after paying the ridiculously tiny bill and thanking
the kindly cook, drove up the lake road and found
a perfect spot in what is now an eighteen hole, pro-designed

golf course, and made love on a grandmotherly quilt,
within a body's length of the cold clear water,
and lay there for an hour in the sun, as naked and at ease
as no one in that place will ever be again.

Beautiful Country

They had five cigarettes going. Also a joint
        and a foot-and-a-half high hookah brimmed
with cannabis above and 3.2 beer below.
        A pale blue smaze hung against the high ceiling.
The six who lived there were lotused around
        four unfolded pages of the *San Antonio Express-*
News, stemming and seeding several resinous pounds of pot,
        three of them still in uniform, fatigues at least,
just back from a day at 'Special Training Detachment,'
        or as it was emblazoned on their helmet liners
'STD' (a sequence of letters not having, in 1971,
        the resonance or implication they have today).
It was a holding company for the hopeless
        and the hopeful. American soldiers, that is, such as they were.
Also in uniform, person number seven. Call him Sergeant Blinks.
        He'd lost an eye in Vietnam, and he was
their dealer, their source, and he liked them more
        than seemed reasonable or right and promised them
each a free nickel bag for their custodial work.
        And even as they worked, he was strapped off and shooting up
with one of the good sterile syringes
        they'd copped from Central Medical Supply.
That was why he liked them, they figured.
        Come home a junkie, he seemed happy
to be here, since they were to have been medics
        and had stolen those syringes long before
Porter developed the bed-wetting problem and Denton
        and Speigel decided they were queers (gay, in those days,
meaning only excessively happy), and before the rest of them
        pleaded not merely ordinary fear
but conscientious objection. They said they meant it, in other words,
        even as they wondered how killing Nixon could be anything but right.

When they could talk at all they had those kinds of conversations.
      They thought about what was wrong and more wrong.
Blinks sat in the room's only chair, spike withdrawn now,
      head lolled off to the side, a kind of fractured baleen
of spittle lip to lip across his open mouth.
      The pot was so sticky they each paused now and then
to work the goo of it up and off each digit, and rolled it
      into black boluses they dropped in a communal coffee cup—
finger hash, it was called, and they couldn't take their eyes off it,
      redolent, drop deadly, and very much desired.
It would be, at the end of their stem-and-seed-parsing,
      what Sergeant Blinks offered in exchange for his lark:
if he could skin-pop them all with a drop or two of his horse
      in the backs of their six left and mostly white hands, it was theirs.
A long pause then. How bad could it be? they wondered.
      Meaning how good. Meaning they wanted what they wanted
and didn't want what they might come to want more
      or too much of, though what was too much
and what did they really want, after all?
      Well, they wanted that cup of finger hash
enough that no one said no, so happily
      Blinks rigged up five new times: syringes
from the dozens in the stolen box,
      a couple cc's from the bent-back cooking spoon,
and then, in between each of the four metacarpal ridges
      across the backs of their newly brave and unheroic hands
he eased—so gently, so skillfully—the needle's slender bevel
      just under the skin and made a series of blisters there,
wens, tear-shaped sebaceous cysts of the same stuff
      he had not long before plunged a pistonful of into his vein.
As per his instructions, they flexed their fists
      and slapped the dabbled backs of their hands
with their undabbled others, and felt come rushing up their arms
      a kind of other-coming, overcoming smolder.
Wilson, the one black man among them, studied his biceps
      and said again and again *hot fudge, hot fudge*.

It was like entering a large perfect mouth,
        a kind of woman-wetness they were up to their shoulders in,
their necks and ears, until there wasn't anything to say
        and even if there had been no mechanism by which to say it.
But it didn't last long, and as far as they would ever know none of them
        did it again. And Blinks left them their nickel bags and the sticky stuff,
and Spiegel boiled up the stems and made iced tea from the water.
        They were so wrecked they forgot to eat and sat
on the sun-busted front porch for hours, watching swallows cruise for moths.
        They even stood to salute at sundown and faced up the block
to the base's back gate at Taps,
        and for some reason this was not at all ironic.
Tra-la they would not kill alas, they would not die.
        They couldn't see the base flag going down,
but the gloaming coming on from the east
        promised another day when everything would be better.
There were bats coming out, hunting.
        America, someone said. Beautiful country.
And it was.

Do Not Go

My father hated loving dogs, since they did so shed,
and messed, chewed, and barked, etcetera too.
Fried chicken neither he did not care for,
it being 'hard to eat', or rather
hard to clean up from. He disapproved of that.
Watermelon, he believed, should with a plate and fork be et.

But lo, he can no longer wash his own car and I cry truly,
so many miles away I cannot wash the thing for him,
though the air cleaner from it even today I would
for a plate underneath a watermelon slab
use and fear of foreign substances not in the least.

But why is it no longer, as in the past, a foreign car, I ask you?
I would ask him but he would agree and seek
therefore a new one, appropriately foreign,
that alas, at his advanced age, in his condition,
he could not, alas, drive, alas. Alas

the long-haired lass I kept undressing night after night
in his backseat years of summer nights ago
like some beautiful sweaty dog shed
so many of her long, long hairs he asked me
was she bald, the poor girl? And I said oh yes, she was,

and he thought, I think, I was just being smart.
But no, I am still very lucky. And all through those years
he kept changing the cars everyone else in the family drove
but him for no reason the rest of us could see
except for maybe dog and girl hair

and some need not the least, we didn't think, acquisitive,
though cars, it seems, are an acquired taste after all and which
I have not myself developed. If the motherfucker just goes, great.
Though not him, oh no, not my mother's lover of cars,
not my father, who since they so shed, hates loving dogs still.

Exxon

Behold the amazing artificial arm, a machine
eerily similar to the arm it replaced, machined
to exacting *tolerances*, as its engineers say,
to 'the limits of allowable error'.
Think of the hand in the glove, the piston
in the cylinder, the cartridge in the chamber
of an arm: a weapon, that is, a firearm,
to say it more primitively, more exactingly,

more ceremonially, and with more appropriate awe.
Behold then the arm from which fire comes, the hand
of a god hurling lightning. Behold the digital trigger, tick of
the finger on the hand separated from its body by the bomb
at the police station, the rifle smoking
just beyond it, as though it might yet shoot again,
the digital tick of the bomb's timer also disembodied now.

Study the artificial arm, its array of hex-
head setscrews, its titanium armatures and axes,
its silicone skins from light pink to dark brown.
Here is this, from the company's catalogue: 'The upper
and lower forearm tubes are secured
to a four-position, manually locked elbow mechanism,'
and this, from God himself, having slain the man's family
and saying to Job, *Or hast thou an arm like God?*

And *Wilt thou also disannul my judgment?*
Wilt thou condemn me, that thou mayest be righteous?
The nerve, and the lack. Beyond the limits of allowable error,
beyond the art of it, the story of Job, the trajectory
of narrative, the flight of the bearings and nails,
the improvised explosive device; beyond war itself, that honored
aesthetic ever-present evil alive and vile in the story
that is a lie about the truth and the truth, great engineer

help us, of the lie. Consider the ongoing
problem of tactile sensitivity, the elusiveness
of feeling, those of us otherwise untouched touched
for several dollars a gallon. And see the soldier in parade dress
easing with his other, non-silicone fingers a credit card into
and removing it rapidly from the slot
in the pump, and entering through its portal
the world of disembodied money

and the exacting tolerances of the world banking
system: behold this soldier, and know of his doubts
about the surrendering of arms, which is to say not only
the ambiguous tolerances of the Second Amendment
but the limb abandoned in Baghdad;
the soldier who has entered also into the system
of government surveillance—the porn sites,
the blogs, the maimed-in-the-line-of-duty

collectorates, the whiskeys and women, the rehabilitations.
See the soldier who nods and whose left
intact hand extended to your extended right one
confuses you an instant, but who nods again
to relieve you in your awkwardness. And behold them,
your untouched touched hands, as he nestles his man-made
right one over both of yours on his left, feeling,
between his old self and his new, a responsible citizen.

Every Night the Long Swim

I miss her, the old dog
dead now more than four years.

She was black and used to dream dreams
that bubbled to the surface of her as she slept.

She preferred the water to the land.
She loved a hand and the way it might be held

from the arm of the chair into the daily air she lived in,
though this world was a long, dry lakelessness

no one in the household but she was so ungilled for.

Thus her dreams.
               Always she seemed to be running,
though I think now she was afloat, and every day

was the duck she offered us. Every night the long swim
over water so dark she disappeared and became the dream,

then swam back, rising,
               shaking away the night into the light
until it was gone.

American Fear

Such as we were we gave ourselves outright.
ROBERT FROST

What it is is a company selling 'clothing
      for the disaffected youth culture',
T-shirts and sweatshirts, mostly black,
      someone's marketing vision for a new world,
a twenty-first century Henry ('You can have
      any color you want so long as it's black') Ford,
that old-time anti-Semite, his going-on-bankrupt
      namesake corporation supplanted by this other.

A button on the website reads 'Ready to Order Fear',
      but everywhere you look it's free: fear of wolves,
bulls, and bears; fear of the sun, fear of that one
      or this one, fear that all it takes is one. Storm fear,
house fear, fear of frost. Fear of gravity is barophobia,
      but there's also Cape Fear, Camp Fear,
and Fear Mountain: you can visit those. There's fear
      of God, fear of the odd; fear of night, fear of air.

Fear of hair is chaetophobia. Eleutherophobia's fear of freedom.
      There's *First Encounter Assault Recon,*
'a survival horror first person shooter, developed
      by Monolith Productions and published by Vivendi',
a video game, a generation's modus vivendi, a way of living
      in which we agree to disagree violently.
Ephebiphobia is the fear of teenagers; melanophobia,
      fear of the color black; caligynephobia,

the fear of beautiful women; and anthrophobia, fear
        of flowers. You can spend hours on a list like this.
Pantophobia is the fear of everything. After two-
        hundred-thirty-odd years the republic crawls
through its slow-motion youth, democracy requiring not
        only equality but a vast sameness many fear,
as some fear guns and others fear their guns
        will be taken away, their beautiful guns,

poetry in them, shining assemblages of articulate parts
        in which ammo is the main idea. Consider the idea
that a thing can be beyond perfection, as in a more perfect
        union, as in the sky and its endlessness
—astrophobia, that's called, the fear of stars
        and celestial space. As for fear of oblivion,
there is no word for it. Come home late, Robert Frost
        rattled the key in the lock and left the door open

until a light was on, a way of allowing what was inside out.
        Later, on his farmhouse porch, Frost trembling,
frightened of the dark, a shotgun in his hands. He thought
        he could talk Khrushchev into nuclear disarmament
(nucleomituphobia, bomb fear) and sulked because
        JFK didn't call him back. The fear of poetry
is metrophobia, and melophobes fear music, cringing
        at the ballgame through 'God Bless America.'

Regarding the disaffected, the *OED* suggests they lack
        first of all affection. Put that with logophobia,
the fear of words, and philophobia, the fear of love.
        Parthenophobia is the fear of virgin girls. WTF
is internet slang and the initials of the World Taekwondo
        Federation, member of the International Olympic Committee.
Why is there is no word for the fear of committees,
        which are so much to be feared? Fear of Germany

is Teutophobia. Vestiphobia is the fear of clothing.
    The fear of flags is vexiphobia. On American Fear's
logo, you can find the flag's stripes resembling a bar code.
    Gringophobia is the fear of Americans, the ones
who fear America ends far north of Tierra del Fuego.
    Fear of a white god is leukotheophobia. A snowclone
is a 'cliché or phrasal template, multi-use, customisable,
        instantly recognisable, time-worn and open

to an array of variants': as in *What Would Henry Ford Do?*
    American Fear's bestselling design:
a mandible-less skull enwreathed by bullets, bunting,
        and feathers, on a base of Fifties-befinned bombs.
There is no word for the fear of growing up,
        though gerascophobia is the fear
of growing old, and old men fear not
        how others might read them by their clothes.

Kings wear robes and senators wear suits. The word senator
        comes from the Latin *senex*, meaning old man,
and gerontophobia is the fear of old people.
    Chronophobia is the fear of time.
Some old men do not wear T-shirts,
        because putting one can be exhausting
and taking it off worse. Imagine fearing a shirt.
    Why is there a word like *bathysiderodromophobia*?

Subways are beautiful in their tunnels and troughs,
        their soiled, palatial stations. 'Go in fear of abstractions,'
Pound said. He suffered not from metrophobia,
        but from madness. To fear in Italian is *temere*.
'What thou lovest well remains, the rest is dross,'
        wrote Pound. 'Better to go down dignified
with boughten friendship at your side than none at all,'
        wrote Frost. He had a lover's quarrel with the world.

Among American Fear's other shirt designs, one called
        'Your Pretty Death Bed', a young woman,
her wrists slashed, looking asleep and covered
        by the stars and stripes. There is no word
for the fear our daughters will commit suicide
        beneath a patriotic blanket. Robert Frost's son, Carol,
shot himself with a deer rifle on October 9, 1940.
        'I took the wrong way with him,' wrote Frost,

who would outlive all but two of his six children.
        A citizen opposes the reintroduction of gray wolves
to the American wilderness, because they are Canadian,
        as though they might harbor within their genes
a disinclination for revolution and a soft spot
        for the queen. Freddie Mercury was a gay British genius
and homophobic sports teams all across the nation sing his
        'We Are the Champions.' He's number 50

among the 100 Greatest Britons, four slots ahead
        of George Harrison, twelve ahead of Jane Austen
and a whopping twenty-three in front of Geoffrey Chaucer.
        Ronald Reagan is number one on the American list.
The only poet in the top twenty-five is Muhammad Ali,
        who comes in just above Rosa Parks but well behind
Elvis, whose pelvis was censored from the television screen.
        No word for the fear of free speech,

but a man was not allowed to board a flight at JFK
        because his T-shirt, in Arabic and English, read
'We will not be silent.' American Fear's shirts
        will not alarm the Transportation Security Administration,
also called the TSA. The fear of silence is sedatephobia.
        The TSA is also the Tourette Syndrome Association,
and based on Boswell's descriptions it is theorised
        that Samuel Johnson suffered from the malady,

making frequent odd grunts and muttering
under his breath 'too, too, too', meaning also
and yes and more, meaning many,
meaning he meant to know all the words,
and the problem with all is everything. All men, all words,
all fears. This beautiful, fearful,
and fearsome country, such as it is,
such as it might yet, someday, become.

After a Rainstorm

Because I have come to the fence at night,
the horses arrive also from their ancient stable.
They let me stroke their long faces, and I note
in the light of the now-emerging moon

how they, a Morgan and a Quarter, have been
by shake-guttered raindrops
spotted around their rumps and thus made
Appaloosas, the ancestral horses of this place.

Maybe because it is night, they are nervous,
or maybe because they too sense
what they have become, they seem
to be waiting for me to say something

to whatever ancient spirits might still abide here,
that they might awaken from this strange dream,
in which there are fences and stables and a man
who doesn't know a single word they understand.

Cemetery Moles

Most are not blind, but still,
might the concrete burial vaults
be perceived before a tunnel
comes to such a sudden hard naught?

Though I notice their mounds mostly
down here with the old stones, last row—
those graves that are not only
vaultless but with a wooden casket too.

And the stories from the sexton?
A filled tooth on a hill whitely shining,
and a mole in a trap one early June,
around its neck a wedding ring.

What Is Yellow About the Yellow Pine?

Not the wood, which is white-to-beige-to-red,
nor the bark, nor the cones, not even the dying needles
gone brown directly from green:

what is yellow is the air around them
in spring, and the wind shadow cast from west to east,
as everything also on the face of the earth

within a mile of a forest of them is washed
by their pollen, paler and purer than saffron.
Everything plucked up from the ground

is likewise silhouetted there, a darkened absence.
Even those of us who sleep
on the other side of screens,

through which passes all night long
their silent, seemingly weightless golden breath:
we rise in the morning and see the sun

as it gleams around the shining rim
of where we lay our individual darknesses down,
the upper halves of us dusted, yellow, shining.

A Lock of Her Hair

As a hoodoo-voodoo, get-you-back-to-me tool,
this hank's thankless task is vast,
a head down to the ground impossibility, possibly,
since what I'm thinking of is your toe pad pinknesses too,
your soup hots and round-and-rounds, the fine
and perfect poundage of you on my paws, the very cause
and problem I moan for and bemoan
the absence of. For Love, above the head
this reddish coil once lavishly wore, there's an air so far away
it's sad for me to even think the same sun's rays play
where it was and do to you what I would do
if I were there or you were here. Still, some thrills
remembered do resemble thrills, one hopes, and the ropes
of it that gently fell around me bound me so well
no hell of miles can defile this dream I dream. I mean
the anyway DNA I can find of you. I mean the home
of bones and blood that holds the whole of you
and which this fizzed-up missive means to conjure, missy,
my world in a curl, girl, this man oh man half man I am
when you're gone.

Campfire

from the journals of D.D. Pye (1871-1890)

For the twigs, being dry and loosely stacked, burned
swiftly, and the kindling, being hewn from a long-standing larch snag,
was also ideally seasoned and crackled brightly into flames.
Then the first small log splits likewise ignited, and I rested there
on my rock, the ever-darkening night cooling the back of my neck
as my face flushed with the glow and heat of the fire.

This was when I chanced to see an ant emerge
from a hole in the smooth bark side of the last length of wood
I had offered to the flames. Although his situation, surely, could not
have been more dire, he seemed calm in his side-to-side explorations
of the log, scurrying away from an edge only once
when a smoke cloud wafted its acrid breath in his face.

By way of experiment, I laid a long slender branch
from the stones of the fire ring to the opposite end of what was both
his potential death-plank and temporary salvation, calculating that,
if resourcefulness and survival ticked as saliently in his jet encasement
as it did within my own skin, he would find this route
to safety eventually. Which he did, but as his bad luck would have it,

from deep within the log he'd perhaps long called home, a pitch pocket,
having reached a temperature from which its brew could no longer expand,
blew with no more than a campfire pop, hardly even a report,
but hard enough to shake from their flaming superstructures
both the log and the bridge I had provided into the flames,
taking the ant as well, whom by now I had in my lonesomeness

become exceedingly glad for, although he was gone in a instant
in the seethe of those coals. This was the point at which I became aware
first of the excessive heat upon my face, so rapt had I been
at my watching, and then, looking up toward the coolness of the night,
aware also of an abundance of stars beyond any man's ability
to reason, let alone cipher or bear, let alone be alone beneath.

Night Music

Full moon and wide forest trail make the headphones possible.
He need not walk by ear but is allowed all the way
to nowhere in particular and back Bach's Brandenburg
concerti, music as lavish and intricate as the pine needle
lacework shadowed along the ground he walks.

What shuffles and skitters, what hoof thumps running
away as he passes, he does not hear, but hears instead
the basso continuo and violins; what inquiries of owl
and crescendo of coyotes he also does not hear, but hears
instead an oboe and French horns calling in his ears.

He fears, therefore, nothing, and allows the day's
wet fallen snow to rumble soundless under his boots
as he walks a mile, and then more, from home.
As many as the stars, the notes of Bach's music,
as many as the Brandenburg's movements, the eyes

he's seen seeing him pass like a kind of God,
which the Margrave of Brandenburg, Bach's benefactor,
was also not, having insufficient musicians to perform
the concerti, and who therefore left the full score unplayed
in his library, until it was sold, upon the Margrave's death,

in 1734, for twenty-four groschen, twenty-four small
silver coins, which end-to-end would barely extend
a quarter the width of the trail our man, deaf to the woods
and the mountain night, walks and even, eventually,
begins to gesture his way down, up, and over, conducting

with his blunt, mittened hands, the virtuoso stars,
an orchestra of light and forest and snow, through which
he walks a mile or more from home, and returns,
so that at the end of concerto number six, we see him bowing
and shaking the hand of the first violinist, the wind.

Which Last

In the thicket just west of my shack,
under the heaviest of canopied pines,

every day, all winter long, two does recline
and rest, and sometimes when I look

from the window their eyes are closed,
but still they go on chewing whatever

snowbound vegetation they've uncovered—
or just their sad, inadequate cuds, I suppose.

As I suppose my daily apple also
is due to them. I've been a little slow to learn

not to throw the core and make them run,
but to toss it gently between us, like so,

then go inside and watch through the glass,
to see which is the lucky first one to it, which last.

Wait

He also finds the wood and steel beautiful,
and the slickness with which all the moving parts
slide open and shut, lifting and lodging
into place the sleek, copper-clad,
steel-jacketed projectile, which, weighing less
than half an ounce, will cover, once

the trigger is pulled, the eighty yards to the doe
in the time it would take him to blink.
He aligns the cross-hairs of the scope
just behind her right shoulder, where the heart
pumps and the lungs, she being absolutely at ease
and grazing, exchange the same mountain air

he also breathes, though he breathes less easily,
since he hopes the single shot will kill her
cleanly and knows, even so, that
should such a clean kill be accomplished, still
he will mourn and be glad simultaneously and will
for the next hour or more be bathed in her blood

and intimate with the then-stilled machinery
of her living—the yards of guts, the probably full
bladder, the buttery liver, and more—nearly all
of which he will leave on the forest floor,
and all of which but the head of her will, he is certain,
be gone within two days, a blessing for the coyotes

and the black and white custodial birds. Even still
he has not yet squeezed the bullet free but breathes
with her to be free of her, allowing each breath
to elongate, allowing himself to see and to note
how the light snow that has been falling
all morning lands on her shoulders

and on the dry last leaves of the shrubs
just behind her and even, though he does not see it,
on the barrel of the rifle itself, some of which,
from the concussion of the shot, will fall away,
and some, due to the fire that accompanies it,
will melt and refreeze as ice as he works on her: the doe

who had discovered so close to the coming winter
the same patch of long and still green mountain fescue
he himself found some weeks ago on a walk, the same day
he found this other spot as well—sheltered, slightly elevated—
from which the fine grass and all ways to it could be seen, the day
he knew all he'd have to do was wait long enough, as he has.

New Poems

(2013)

Slow Dreams

All my life I have been bothered by them,
these glacial enactments and thickened plots,
these head dense molassical happenings
all plodding exposition or instant, endless crisis.
In my daughter's dreams whole civilisations fall,
entire oeuvres jet from the pens of poets
as they pass across her patient dream screen,
from their mothers' breasts to the corner
of Westminster Abbey in an eye's rapid blink.
Here comes the sun announcing not what's next
but never is. I want to say, O Mother, why
that bloody knife in your hands? Or you, naked
stranger, what were you about to do? This morning
my daughter announces that my granddaughter,
who does not yet exist, was last night elected president
of a country where only women ride horses,
and this after the war between the last two
believers in God—when she stops and asks me
what of my dreams? what worlds have I seen?
what miracles and vast historical tableaux?
And as always I sigh, and dredge it forth,
some paltry, not even anecdotal sliver:
the way paper waves gusher off west and east
from the archetypal mouth of a scissors;
the tome of unclench, the very continental drift
of a single kiss beginning to end;
my own utterly familiar hands approaching me,
coming straight at my face and filled
with water that no matter how long held
never completely spills. My thirst.

Religion

The last thing the old dog brought home
from her pilgrimages through the woods
was a man's dress shoe, a black, still-shiny wing-tip.

I feared at first a foot might be in it.
But no, it was just an ordinary shoe.
And while it was clear it had been worn,

and because the mouth of the dog—
a retriever, skilled at returning ducks and geese—
was soft, the shoe remained a good shoe

and I might have given it
to a one-legged friend
but all of them dressed their prostheses too,

so there it was. A rescued
or a stolen odd shoe. Though in the last months
of the dog's life, I noticed

how the shoe became her friend, almost,
something she slept on or near
and nosed whenever she passed,

as though checking it to see if,
in her absence, that mysterious, familiar,
missing foot, might not have come again.

For One Who Prays for Me

I do not wish to hurt her, who loves me
and who asks for me only every blossom and more,

but in fact, when I say God I mean the wind
and the clouds that are its angels;

I mean the sea and its enormous restraint,
all its fish and krill just the luster of a heavenly gown.

And while it is true there are days when I think
something more must be in the wind than air, still I believe

the afterlife is dirt, but sweet, and heaven's coming back
in the lewd, bewhiskered tongue of an iris.

The River Itself

It takes him a week, maybe nine days,
he can't remember now, moving upriver
all the while, and mapless, making
the judgments others before him had made—
meaning no tributary streams, no east, west,
south, or north forks, but the river itself—
and then the lake in the higher mountains
and the largest of its inlet streams,
the pond, the brook, the tule-thick tarn,
the rivulet and horsetail waterfall, all the way
to the man-sized final slab of melting ice
stoppered in the gash just north of the peak
that goes by the same name as the river,
from which he calls hello, hello to the rain.

A Photograph of Philip Levine on the Brooklyn Promenade, May 2000, Lower Manhattan in the Background

Arthur Lieberman, the cousin in Levine's poem,
turned to watch the day's last light subsiding
over the East River and suffered...what?
An attack? a premonition? His son, falling
to the Manhattan streets on Black Thursday, 1929.
It was coming and no one knew. García Lorca and Hart Crane,
said to be in the room, did not know their ends either.

And when I saw this picture of Levine
in a magazine I might not have wanted
otherwise, I did not think of Lorca
or Crane, or the horrified, good cousin,
Arthur Lieberman. I just wanted the picture.
Even the interview, I must admit,
did not really matter, the poet's words

as spoken prose not so fine a thing as the poems
or the picture: and the picture, a monochromatic
mid–spring day in May, the sky to the west
that pale gray of pigeons' underbellies,
skyline receding to the softer blur
that is distance through a telephoto lens.
And what Levine sees, leaned against

the elegant iron fence, we can only guess:
the air above far Coney Island or Canarsie Beach?
a woman conducting the wind? a pair of pigeons
blown from the sidewalks like a blessing?
He looks to the southeast: south for Crane,
flailing in the water behind the boat
from Veracruz; and east for Lorca,

gunned down by Falangists in Spain.
Such are the cardinal points—madness and politics—
compass routes from everywhere else
to here, the North, South, East, and West
of where we're going and where we are.
And it isn't just knowing that the East River
is out of sight behind him, or that the fence

he leans against comes close to running
true north, or that the blurred towers to the west,
because the camera's eye cannot see two places
at once, only seem, on this gray day, May, 2000,
to be turning into ghosts already, already half gone.
I was drawn instead by the sadness in the man's eyes,
believing it the ghosts of Whitman, Lorca, and Crane,

angels of the poet's long devotion.
And when I called Brooklyn, that Wednesday,
September 12, 2001, Levine was asleep, so I spoke instead
to his wife, to Frannie, who could only say
that they had watched. I was far away, but looking
at the picture as we talked, and I could see in it
the way they must have headed home after a while,

arm in arm, and I understood how you could
fall in love forever with someone or something
that would never be the same—a photograph, a poem:
Levine's eyes mourning Lorca and Crane then,
and the others now, the ones whose loss
he watched from the Brooklyn Promenade,
with Frannie, until they could bear to see no more.

At the Beginning of Another War

March 19, 2003

Under a faded wooden soda crate filled almost
with twenty-three dusty amber bottles;
in a slanted, half-collapsed
cardboard box; among cracked terra cotta pots
and an oily, filth-encrusted hydraulic jack,
I found the plaster cast of a man's erect phallus.
It was not unimpressive in its way,
though possessed finally of ordinary dimensions,
neither a pornmaster's swag nor the Dillinger of myth.
I thought about it hard, so to speak, and held it up
and noticed at the base—a sort of scrotal blob
mashed down flat—words:
'*Abner & Daisy May, Baker, Oregon*', and a date.
And what a date it must have been. '*December 9, 1941.*'
Men were lining up to kill and die
for all the reasons you and I know even now made sense
a little, as much as things like that ever do.
And here was this thing among a host of other useful tools,
but it was what I wanted.
Surely these were not their real names, neither his
nom de guerre, the halfway prettified
euphemism she might have given to what it was
they memorialised that day and made the most of
before he left. And surely she was not entirely the flower
he would have whispered to, nor even the verb
her there-inscribed middle name asked before they did
this thing that might well have outlived them both.
I assure you, it was hard
buying it I mean, there being both the blue-haired proprietor
and no price tag either.
'Oh my,' she said, 'where did you find this?'
and all I did was point, wordless, while she swaddled it

in a wad of newspapers without ever once
letting her fingers touch its surface,
then shoved it in an old grocery bag: one dollar.
Fifty miles north I stopped where Joseph Canyon
opens out a thousand feet deep to the east.
It was not December but March. The canyon walls were
adorned with a billion early balsamroot blossoms,
almost daisy-like, an unsullied buttery yellow.
My first thought was to hurl it like a hand grenade
down onto the scree and talus
just to see it explode, but I couldn't do it.
Instead, I followed a deer trail down, and another after that,
deeper into the canyon than any arm ever could have thrown it,
and in the shade of an ancient, enormous yellow pine
twice scribed by lightning from crown to the ground
buried it in a cairn of jagged but stackable basalt.
But not before holding it, presenting it before me,
as I thought he might have, and holding it also
as I believed she would, and even, I confess,
offering it, before I left, in honor of them who made it,
more than one goodbye kiss.

Letter to a Young Poet

In the biographies of Rilke, you get the feeling
you also get now and then in the poems
that here, surely, is a man among the archetypes of all men
you'd rather hang than have notice your daughter.
And yet, how not to admire the pure oceanic illogic
of his arguments, those preposterous
if irremediable verities. It can't be helped. They're true.
And there's no other word for him, for whom sadness is
a kind of foreplay, for whom seduction
is the by-product of the least practical art there is.
Those titanic skills in language, the knack lacked by
every other lung-driven swimmer through the waters
of lexicon, in spite of the fierce gravities of all grammar
and the sad, utilitarian wallflowers of usage:
well, there you go, my half-assed angel, that's your challenge.
Beethoven believed he was homely too, but you
must understand: Rilke's tools you can pick up, every one
but the one they all share. Even Stevens,
who must have known an actuary or two and still for whom
the brown salt skin of order sang beyond and in the ache
of longing. And Celan, whose most terrible angels
rang him like a bell of rings. And Whitman,
dandy of the cocked hat and tilted head himself,
the gentlest, the gentile Jew, the jubilant lonely grubber
eyeing the grocery boy. Inside
them all, a man, if you could help it,
you would never consent to become,
except if only, just for once, you could be him.

Civics

Seven wild turkeys have assembled
under the canopy of the biggest pine
just north of the house. They tremble-
quiver violently now and then,

to shake the snow away, then go on
sleeping. Though until they do they resemble
a cluster of god eggs or snow-covered, holy stones,
or better yet the cherished ceremonial bells

somewhere—a government hall, a cathedral—
that some yawning functionary has to tend
and, by virtue of a forgotten decree and a call,
must ring, for some reason, again and again.

Mouth

When she bought the thrift shop ventriloquist's dummy,
she said, Who could resist him? and it was true,
a little man who'd sit on your lap
and say the things your lips should not.
And they were expensive, these things, custom
made, she believed, though that was what
at last began to bother her about him:
the coiffed black hair, the pencil mustache,
his diminutive, excellent tuxedo,
like a dollhouse playboy or a maitre d' nose high
to the place setting. It wasn't so much
how he looked drolly on as she made love
with a larger if less wooden man, but that
she'd sometimes think to sit him on her bare thigh
afterward as he reviewed his competitor's performance.
And it wasn't that her hand inside him made her,
or him, or them, cruel exactly, or even unkind,
though there were sighs she could fake
and words he would not. It wasn't even the lover
who took him by the throat and tossed him face first
back on his corner chair and then took her again,
and harder, nor that as he did she imagined
the fleshly man the dummy, the taste
of his sweat the dummy's sweat, the smell
of his dangerous rage the source of the words
only the dummy could utter. No. It was,
she insisted, the mouth nothing ever entered
but from within, and how she could open that mouth
all the way and tilt back the empty head of him
and laugh, and laugh, from the gut, from the heart,
which was nothing more or less than her fist.

News

There's a mountain and a hundred miles
between me and the jazz station, but sometimes
I can live with the static, a kind of extra-tempo
air-drum percussion, the dead singer's voice
tanged by smokes and too much gin. Some days,
all I want is no news, none of the time.

On the other hand, this afternoon it wasn't music
pulled me up, but what the field guide calls
the black-chinned hummingbird's 'thin, excited chippering'.
It had got itself trapped in the garage, and though
the big door was open, it stayed in the window
through which it could clearly see a world.

By the time I heard it, it was so exhausted
it let itself be cupped in my slow man's hands,
and emitted, as I closed it in, a single chip then silence.
At the edge of the woods I knelt and opened my hands.
Not even thumb-thick, its body pulsed with breath,
its wings spread across my palm, its eyelash legs

sprawled left and right, indecorously. I stroked it
as lightly as I could, as I might not my lover's breast
but the down made seemingly of air thereon, and twice.
Then it flew, a slow lilt into the distance. For a while,
even peace seemed possible, in the background
Billie Holiday singing 'Strange Fruit'.

While You Were Out of Town

I left the man with the steam cleaner all alone
in the house and watched from my shack
as he poured bucket by bucket the gray
brackish water that had rinsed our comings
and goings from the carpet. That morning I had moved

all the small items—hassock, coffee table, magazine rack,
and more—to the hardwood and tile to make way
for his work. Also the two end tables, the floor lamp—
everything one man could lift by himself,
even the dog's toys and the window shade ropes.

And I would have noticed, had it been on the floor,
your black lacy bra, hanging by a strap
from a dresser handle, but I'm sorry, there it was,
after he left, still hanging, though I noticed it hung this time
by the left shoulder instead of the right,

as though it had fallen as he cleaned the alley
next to your side of the bed, that trouble spot
where the dog sleeps. Yes, that's it, I'm sure,
it had fallen, and he, in one professional motion,
had put it back, as I had put it back

just the night before, having noted—
for whatever reason one might note such a thing,
even before I held it to my lips
and took in the rich, cool scent of your absence—
which seemingly negligent strap it dangled by.

Morelity

Heavy thatch of leaf and needle,
     sun-mottled also,
so the eye you need to find them
     almost always fails.

But when you do, their dark knuckles
     rucking up the duff,
their airy reticular brains
     bobbing in the air

and breathing a sexual musk—
     after that they're everywhere.
Your grocery bag grows as heavy
     as a child, and limp,

as if plucked up they could only sleep
     and dream, of how the sun
they had yearned for awaits them
     in the butter's slick

and a skillet's sublunary
     bed, where they'll sizzle
from fungal unto meat
     which you will take and eat.

Apology

Just moments before the dogs and I came
around the blind, climbing curve, you must have
leaned your bike against the tree and peeled
the spandex riding shorts down and squatted.
Really, I would have turned away but for the dogs,
who barked and ran at you and nosed you too, I fear,
as you stayed, then quickly wiped, and tossed away
a pale white rose of tissue before standing.
There remained then the momentary difficulty
of sweat-wet shorts pulled up, a sort of
push and sway of roundnesses and nylon
I will not further describe. Instead
you should know that, as it seemed you preferred,
I never saw your face, though you must have
glanced around at the sound of the dogs' bark
and seen me there as well. Forgive me what
I did see and did not turn away from,
what I could not now or ever know you by
anywhere, though it is also true I will never forget.
Know also, that in your haste to be gone,
after your hard pumping strokes took you
out of sight beyond the next bend, I saw
the tissue there, on the old road's rocky verge,
and therefore shooed the dogs away and touched
its filmy petal edge with a match.
I stayed until it almost all had burned,
then twist-crushed it under my bootsole,
that there be no evidence left, no litter,
and after a rain or two not even scent enough
to make the dogs take note again, although
this morning, making breakfast, I noticed
how it all came back to me—in a cloud

or a wind, in a dog's quiet lapping
at her dish, in the shadow of my hand
harshly cast, or the coffee's dark smell of smoke.
And I stood there for a while, empty cup
held before me, as the sun rose full on
and my wife came in and caught me blushing.

Mammoth

Returning the refilled feeder to its hanger on the tree,
I am followed, and from my first step out the door
to the careful slipping of the loop of twine over the hook's tang
made to understand—as he darts within inches of my eyes—
that this hummingbird, while he may not despise me,
finds my human dawdling not simply unacceptable but offensive,
a lumbering no less appalling than the billion plumbable pores
of my moonscape face. Even the vast tidal wash
of my infernal, slow-witted breathing disgusts him. Therefore he loops
so swiftly around me I can hardly blink, and when I tell him he is
beautiful, he hears only the two ton roar of a wooly mammoth
as it thrashes in a bog, at the edges of which, this time of year,
the red, sweet flowers he loves most of all still thrive.

Babel

The language he speaks and writes is spoken
and written by no one but him, which solves,
for him at least, the problem of audience,
unless somehow, against the odds, he believes

there is someone to whom his alphabet speaks,
his words, if they are words and not notes
of some other sort of singing, a system of clicks
and impossible vowels, the strange habitats

in which his bent and prickly syllables live.
The patience with which he clears his throat
and nods to us and begins, mild and tentative
at first, to read, or sing, or ceremonially recite

the epic of his people or the story of his God
or the description of his lost beloved's body,
moves us so each time, we concentrate and nod
but understand nothing at all of what he

has said. And when he's finished and looks at us,
expectantly, we, in our own inadequate tongues
and often gesticulating wildly, discuss
the majesty of his accomplishment, which no one

fathoms any part of, least of all our praise,
if that's what it is, since we too are the last
or perhaps even the only ones ever to raise
into the air such utterances—from the past

or the future or from this very moment in time,
when no one knows what anyone means to say or tell,
not even at night, when we seem to pray, then recline
on our bunks, each in his own terrible, familiar cell,

with the toilet and the nightlight, with the reams
of paper, filled and yet to be, that surround us,
and he goes on speaking through our dreams,
where everything, making sense, astounds us.

Triage

Scarred by a long gone buck's rubbing,
shoved westward by his develveting grind,
the aspen had always leaned, and I had thought
many times I should stake it up, straighten it out,

but I never did, then last week's several heavy
feet of snow became rain, and under that weight it split
at the buck's scar and bent to the ground,
and I was bereft. But in my regret I hauled

through the snow a hundred feet of ropes,
a come-along, a pair of steel pintel hooks,
and a five-gallon bucket of hopeful arborist's
paraphernalia. I tied it off to a stouter tree,

winched it upright again, braced it with a two-by-four
plank notched and swaddled at the notched end
in innertube ribbons, then guyed it off to the fir
that was the engine of its reascension.

Afterward I plastered black tar around its wound,
wound a bandage of grafting tape over the tar,
and covered the tape in a green vinyl sleeve
against the winter yet to come. And every day

in order to offer such apologies as I can
I visit it. Sometimes, like the other day, I sit with it,
put an arm around it, and describe the motions
of its leaves in spring and summer,

and especially in its glorious fall:
how its gold shimmers, and sometimes how
a leaf will loose itself and fly the ten yards
to the porch of my shack and settle on a chair,

or, in the cold October rains, plaster itself
to a window like a kiss. That day I also explained
the next step in our treatment. How once
it is leafed out and green again, I will,

using the same rope that righted it, fasten
that rope at the height of my knee, at the strong
unbroken butt of it just below the buck's black scar,
and winch it a bit more upright yet, until,

by high summer, as straight as nearly any tree
around it, it will stand. Soon the seat of my pants
was wet from the snow and I was shivering,
but still I didn't want to go. I stood

and stroked the dressing around its wound
and resolved to come back from my shack
that afternoon, to read it a poem or two—
not my own, certainly not this one—but maybe

'The Wellfleet Whale' or 'The Trees',
in which 'their greenness is a kind of grief',
though I have not done so yet. 'Begin afresh,'
I think this afternoon. 'Last year is dead.'

Larkin, I think, would have thought me a fool,
Kunitz, maybe not so much. Though I notice
in the divot where I'd sat beside it, a puddle
my own face regards me from. I'm empty-handed

and know neither poem, the short nor the long,
by heart. Only end of the Kunitz: 'like us,' it goes,
'disgraced and mortal,' from the puddle, says my face.

Cenotaph

Never especially inclined mathematically, my father,
days past his eightieth birthday, calculated the following:

if all the names of the dead, military and civilian alike,
of every nationality, from his war—the good one—

were blasted into granite, as were those
of the American soldiers who had perished in the bad one, mine,

the resulting monument would be almost a mile long
and a hundred feet deep. Setting aside the engineering challenges,

he believed the greater problem was the names: sixty million,
he ciphered, though I don't know how. His imagined monument,

a project no greater than the interstate highway system
or the dams across the nation's rivers, could take decades

to erect. No more than Rushmore or Crazy Horse,
and yet who would have envisioned such a task?

But I remember how, the night of the first moon landing,
he stood in his backyard in the heart of the heart of the country,

straining through binoculars to see what could not be seen
but was. Now, ten years past his monumental calculations,

the only numeral that matters to him is 2. We are not sure why.
Perhaps because my twin sister and I are two. As are he

and our mother, her failing eyes and gentle hands. Therefore
'two' is the answer to every problem the young neurologist asks,

a physician not much older than my own children,
none of whom ever lived through something called the draft.

My father does not know what year we are in or the name
of our current president. Even the names of his grandchildren

are sometimes lost to him, and if we were to ask
that name by which he calls himself, we fear that, too,

may be gone. He does not know, and probably never did,
the word *cenotaph*, though the memorial he once imagined

would have been just that, an empty tomb.
O, Father, my father, let me estimate the dead for you:

it has been and will be everyone. Let us understand
that mountains are—like plains and swamps,

like rivers and oceans—death and life factories, forges from which
come numberless souls, residents on a spinning blue cenotaph

that without us has no name nor need of one.
These were the dead of a single war, these the dead

of the others. And here are those who died, as we say, in peace,
some whose lives have faded within them until they are

only the names and numbers they had been known by.
And here is where they were, beneath a cyclical moon,

which bears through the universe some footprints and a flag.

Soundings

The birdhouse made from a gourd is wired
to a flanged loop of steel and screwed to the southeast post
of the shack. Two holes at the top—near where the stem was,
for a thong of leather to hang it by, which long ago broke—
are now the fingerholes of the mournful wind instrument it's become.
The broad round bowl of it makes a sort of birdly
basso profundo that pearls through the steel, into the post,
the floor joists and walls in two notes: a slightly sharp D
and an equally sharp F, says the guitar tuner,
which explains why all my thinking these days
is in B-flat, a difficult key for all but the clarinet
and this sudden covey of nuthatches, whose collective woe
makes it a minor chord I am in the middle of.
Nothing to do but hoist such silks as the luff
of limbs and needles suggests, and sail on,
the barely-escaped-from-the-cat chipmunk chattering
like a gull, and the mountain's last drift of snow
resembling the back of a sounding whale. Hear the thrum of the rigging,
Daggoo? Hear its profoundest woo, its sensible gobbledy-goo
and doo-wop, the boo-hoos of the spheres, by vectors and veers,
by tacks and refractal jabberings, taking us deeper into the weirdness
of the ghost sea those prairie hills were the bottom of once,
this nowhere we shall not be returning from.
Draw the lines! Assume the crow's nest, Pip. This ship
sails on music and wind, and away with birds.

Stop and Listen

Sometimes the woods at night are so still
the sound of your own breath
abashes you, to say nothing
of the racket as you walk.

Sometimes talking helps, saying
a poem, or even, if you're going downhill,
singing. Other times there's nothing
to do but stop and listen, or even sit

and close your eyes in the name
of attentiveness. In daylight,
there are birds, and for some reason
the wind too is always awake,

delivering weather or dust.
At night, you concentrate,
your listening is enhanced,
and sooner or later you will hear

a scale of bark let loose from a tree
or a needle tick from limb to limb
on its enormous journey to the earth.
And sometimes, having resumed

your walk, you will stop at the top
of the ridge above your house.
Its window lights will illumine the ground
around it, and you will listen again

and hear the faint hum of it—
the buzz of its light bulbs, the industry
of its clocks. And sometimes
you will approach it as would a thief

and peer through the windows,
in order that you might covet,
being part of the world's greater silence,
everything that is already yours.

Anatomy of Melancholy

Lucy Doolin, first day on the job, stroked his goatee
and informed the seven of us in his charge
his name was short for Lucifer, and that his father, a man
he never knew, had been possessed,
as his mother had told him, of both an odd sense of humor
and a deep and immitigable bitterness. Also
that the same man had named Lucy's twin brother,
born dead, Jesus Christ. These facts, he said,
along with his tattoos and Mohawked black hair,
we should, in our toils on his behalf, remember.

As we should also always remember to call him
only by that otherwise most womanly diminutive,
and never, he warned, by his given nor surname,
least of all with the title 'mister' attached,
which would remind him of that same most hated father
and plunge him therefore into a mood
he could not promise he would, he said, 'behave
appropriately within'. Fortunately, our job,
unlike the social difficulties attached thereto,
was simple: collect the trash from county's back roads.

Although, given Lucy's insistence on thoroughness,
this meant not only beer cans and bottles,
all manner of cast-off paper and plastics, but also
the occasional condom too, as well as the festering
road-kill fresh and ridden with maggotry,
or desiccate and liftable only from the hot summer tar
with a square-bladed shovel, all of which was to be tossed
into the bed of the township flat-bed truck we ourselves
rode to and from the job in. By fifty-yard increments
then we traveled. He was never not smoking a cigarette.

Late every afternoon, at the dump, while we unloaded
our tonnage of trash, he sat with Stump McCarriston,
sexton of the dump and the dump's constant resident,
in the shade, next to a green, decrepit trailer
we marveled at and strangely envied, since every inch
of wall we could see through the open door
was plastered with fold-outs and pages
from every Stump-salvaged *Playboy* and nudie magazine
he had ever found among the wreckage there.
Stump, we understood, was the ugliest man on earth.

Even had Lucy not told us so, we would have known,
by the olfactory rudeness within twenty yards
of his hovel, that he never bathed. And once,
while we shoveled and scraped, he took up the .22
from the rack beside his door and popped
with amazing accuracy three rats not fifty feet from us,
then walked to their carcasses, skinned them out,
and hung their hides on a scavenged grocery store rack
to dry. He was making, Lucy explained, a rat hide
coat we could see, come the fall, except for school.

As for school, it was a concept Stump could not fathom
and Lucy had no use for, on the truck's dash
all that summer Robert Burton's *Anatomy of Melancholy*,
a tome he said he'd read already eleven times,
this summer being the twelfth. We thought, in some way,
it might have had to do with something like the gallery
Stump's trailer contained, the first word of its title
meaning something to us, the last nothing at all.
There were things about men we might be
unable ever to know, but which we somehow knew was lucky.

And Lucky, incidentally, was the name of the cat,
fat and mangey, that, once Stump was back in the shade
with Lucy, began, one by one, to consume the hideless rats.
The town we came from was sinking into the emptiness
of a thousand abandoned coal mine shafts beneath it,
and rats were more common than hares
and universally despised. They shamed us, it seemed,
as we were shamed by ignorance and curiosity—
the bodies of those women on the walls, the provenance
of rats the very earth offered up like a plague,

the burden of a name like Lucifer or Stump,
whose name, as it was scrawled on his mailbox,
seemed to be Stumplin Reilly McCarriston, Esquire.
Of the seven of us, one would die in Vietnam,
one, after medical school, would hang himself
from a beam in his parents' basement, the others
merely gone, vanished in actuality if not in memory.
Leaving me, alone, to tell this story. How Stump
would spend his last twenty years in prison,
having shot Lucy—one slender, flattening .22 slug

through the forehead—as he stood fifty feet away,
balanced atop the tub of an ancient wringer washer,
arms extended, like Jesus Christ, said Stump,
whose trailer was bulldozed into the dump itself
even before the trial, and who, no doubt, by some
court-appointed lawyer if not the appalled sheriff himself,
was forced to bathe and shave, to step into the unknown country
of a scentless white shirt and black, businessman's trousers,
in order to offer his only yet most sincere defense,
that Lucifer—Mr Doolin, as the court insisted—had told him to.

Index

Index of titles and first lines

(Titles and sub-titles are shown in italics, first lines in roman type.)